The Disappearing Sexes

BOOKS BY ROBERT P. ODENWALD

Your Child's World
The Disappearing Sexes

Robert P. Odenwald, M.D.

THE
Disappearing
SEXES

Random House, New York

FIRST PRINTING

The author is grateful for permission to reprint excerpts from the following:

From CRISIS IN BLACK AND WHITE by Charles E. Silberman. © Copyright 1964 by Random House, Inc.

From THE SECOND SEX by Simone de Beauvoir, Trans. by H. M. Parshley. Copyright 1952 by Alfred A. Knopf, Inc. Reprinted by permission of Alfred A. Knopf, Inc. and Jonathan Cape Ltd.

From THE SIXTH MAN by Jess Stearn. © Copyright 1961 by Jess Stearn. Reprinted by permission of Doubleday & Company, Inc. and the Sterling Lord Agency.

From THE COMPLETE BOOK OF BIRTH CONTROL (Ballantine Books). © Copyright 1961 by Dr. Alan S. Guttmacher, Winfield Best and Frederick S. Jaffe.

From THE FAMILY IN A MONEY WORLD by Frances Lomas Feldman. © Copyright 1957. Reprinted by permission of Family Service Association of America.

From KIDS, CRIME, AND CHAOS by Roul Tunley. © Copyright 1962 by Roul Tunley. Reprinted by permission of Harper & Row, Publishers.

From OUT OF WEDLOCK by Leontine Young. Copyright 1954 by McGraw-Hill, Inc. Used by permission of McGraw-Hill Book Company.

From AND GOD MADE MAN AND WOMAN by Lucius F. Cervantes, S.J. Henry Regnery Co., Chicago, Illinois.

From an article, DESCRIPTION OF THE FORT GREENE HOUSING DEVELOPMENT IN BROOKLYN by William Longgood. Copyright 1964 by the World-Telegram and Sun.

From WHO KILLED ROMANCE? by Elaine Kendall. © 1963 by Elaine Kendall. This piece originally appeared in the February 1963 issue of Mademoiselle magazine. Reprinted by permission of the Sterling Lord Agency.

Excerpt from the report on homosexuality by the Committee on Public Health of The New York Academy of Medicine. Reprinted by permission of the Committee on Public Health.

A C K N O W L E D G M E N T S :

This work is based on speeches, writings and psychiatric experiences; it represents a synthesis of training and experience over many years both in this country and abroad. I wish therefore to acknowledge my indebtedness to teachers, colleagues and patients who have contributed to the present understanding which this work reflects. It is obviously impossible to mention all by name, but the gratitude exists.

For his valued help in preparing the manuscript, I especially wish to thank John L. Springer, who, through his generous and intelligent assistance, made the writing of this book possible.

Table of Contents

The Disappearing Sexes

1

THE
DECLINE
OF
SEX

WE ARE UNDERGOING A CHANGE IN THE RELATIONSHIPS OF THE sexes as profound as any in the world of science or warfare. We are experiencing no less than a revolution in our attitudes toward sex, as most humans have understood it since the beginning of time. We are raising a race of less masculine men and less feminine women, and we are in danger, if this trend continues, of developing a population of neutrals with virtually nothing to distinguish them but the shape and size of their breasts and genitals. As we shall see, this development is the source of many great social evils—sexual promiscuity, juvenile delinquency, homosexuality and others.

[3]

Many factors are working to eliminate differences between the sexes. Perhaps foremost is the belated recognition that woman is not, after all, the inferior sex; that she has intellectual capabilities far beyond those with which she has been credited. However, in striving to prove that women are equal to men, many moderns are saying that women are very little different from men.

Another factor, less widely recognized, is the radical modification of the structure of family life. In America particularly, where the trend toward the neutralization of the sexes is most pronounced, family life has ceased to be an experience shared by parents and children *plus* grandparents, uncles, aunts, cousins and second cousins. It is no longer the traditional group relationship in which men perform some specific tasks while women perform others. Rather, it is an operation in which Daddy may wash the dishes and the clothes while Mommy works in the factory on the night shift and the children see visible proof that she wears the pants.

Still another factor is the revolution in sexual morality in the twentieth century. Many of the traditional distinctions concerning the acceptable conduct of men and women were rooted in the belief that pregnancy inevitably resulted from sexual intercourse. The development of effective contraceptives and the spreading notion that everyone has a right to sexual fulfillment have torn down many safeguards around girls that formerly made their training very different from that accorded boys.

These and many other factors are profoundly affecting modern boys' conception of the duties and responsibilities that will be theirs in manhood, and girls' understanding of their obligations as mature women. We are moving toward a one-sex society.

When I remark that differences between the sexes are disappearing at an alarming rate, I am likely to get a response like this: "So what? Almost all the so-called differences are artificial anyway. They're a result of the way we've been brought up—environmental influences."

This is a belief now held by many women, who can wear pants and stand at a bar to drink alone if they choose to, and who fight not only to hold jobs on an equal basis with men, but also to enjoy the unlimited sexual freedom they think men have.

As we watch the steady trend toward the neutrality of the sexes, this question is crucial: Are men and women basically made the same way except for obvious differences in the size and shape of their sex organs? If the answer is yes, I am crying over nothing, and we would be better off getting rid of our outmoded notions.

On this point, however, the scientific evidence cannot be disputed. A woman is more than just a man who happens to have enlarged breasts and no penis. She is different in every part of her body—so much so, in fact, that one can take any cell from a human being and determine whether it came from a male or a female. Moreover, one can look at a human skeleton, or even a small section of one, and—as the late Dr. Ales Hrelicka, anthropologist of the Smithsonian Institution, pointed out—make a correct diagnosis of sex. And this is equally true of skeletons thousands of years old.

As might be expected, the hormonal composition of males and females is likewise vastly different. When male glands were implanted in a female guinea pig which had been castrated, it not only began to look like a male but also began to chase females in heat.

As Freud said, "anatomy is destiny." Even when a boy and girl are exposed to identical environmental experiences, the boy will usually grow taller than the female, heavier, and with more muscle on his body, while she will develop more fat. His different hand structure will enable him to lift weightier objects and to squeeze them more intensely than she can. She will be relatively taller from the waist up; her neck, legs, arms and thumbs will be shorter but her head, trunk and index fingers will be longer. He will have a larger dome, a larger nose and a more conspicuous chin.

Their metabolism also will be different. He will need different kinds of food because his body will burn fuel faster than hers will. He will use the air he breathes in a different way and in many stages will exhale much more carbon dioxide. His blood is different; there will be proportionately many more red corpuscles in it than in hers.

While many mannerisms of men and women can be attributed to how they are brought up and what their parents and society expect of them, nevertheless greatly different temperaments and drives are inherently characteristic of each sex. Dr. Benjamin Spock —who has probably seen as many babies and young children as anyone else in the world—says that the typical boy shows a much greater restlessness and striving from birth than does his sister, and that boys are more resistant to authority and less receptive to order. For example, a girl can be taught to use the toilet earlier and with fewer setbacks. Dr. Spock says that even year-old boys display a much greater interest in mechanical things than do year-old girls, and at the age of two or three years boys take much more readily to games involving pretended gunplay and acts of violence. The boy who chooses to play cowboys and Indians and the girl who prefers to play with dolls are not the products of environment,

[6]

because at such early ages they have not been taught what society expects of them; rather they are doing what comes naturally to them. I can confirm Dr. Spock's observations from my own experiences in treating young boys and girls.

Differences between the sexes extend into the psychological realm and may be more important here than anywhere else. For instance, while women are not less intelligent than men, their cast of mind is distinctly different. Generally speaking, men take the broad view of things and tend to abstract thinking, while women concentrate on details and particulars. Women are usually much more sensitive than men to the emotional undercurrents in a situation and often respond emotionally to conditions that men do not even notice. This is one reason why, in my practice, I hear the complaint, "So-and-so hurt my feelings," more often from women than from men, and it is also why women are more likely to make love the center of their lives. By contrast, men tend to focus their attention on work, and love exists only on the periphery of things.

The act of sexual intercourse dramatizes the deeply rooted differences between the sexes. Nature has fashioned the bodies of male and female so that he is the aggressor. The sex act is impossible unless he is psychologically and physically disposed to engage in it. On the other hand, the woman can never play more than a subordinate role. At most, she can stimulate her husband so he becomes desirous of intercourse. But if he cannot or will not be stimulated, all her efforts are in vain.

Moreover, nature has so arranged things that if he is determined to have intercourse against her wishes, he can force his way into her body. But if she is determined to have it and he does not cooperate, the act is impossible.

No matter how much we talk about equality of the sexes, this vital fact exists and will continue to exist as long as men and women are made as they are. It is true that a woman can be indifferent or tell her husband that she does not want him to touch her. But if she holds him off in this fashion, it is through an emotional or moral dominance that has been developed—not a physical one that exists naturally.

Are the psychological and emotional differences of women and men the result of upbringing and training? This question is much debated. It is true that to a certain extent the emotional reactions of men and women are distinctive simply because they act as they are expected to act. A girl inclined to be rough in manner and something of a tomboy will be told thousands of times that she is not "acting like a lady." The boy who likes to play games with girls will be derided as a sissy and taught in countless ways that his conduct is unbecoming.

But this fact does not quite justify the currently fashionable belief that women are the way they are only because that is how they have been trained. Those who maintain that emotional and intellectual differences between the sexes are the results of training, rather than innate characteristics, put the relationship in the wrong order. Rather than differences being the result of training, the training is the result of differences.

Here we have the collective wisdom of mankind to instruct us. Since men and women began their relationship with a clean slate, the tradition that women perform certain functions and men perform others must have grown out of their very natures. It is inconceivable that at some time in the past men got together and decided that this was how things would be. Rather than resulting from an arbitrary decision by males, differences in function (apart

[8]

from those clearly imposed by nature) seem to have sprung from the very needs of the sexes involved.

Marriage can be defined as a relation of one or more men to one or more women, recognized by custom or law, and establishing certain privileges and duties both for the parties entering the union and for children born in it. But marriage is more than a regulated sexual relation. It is an economic institution affecting the rights of all members of the family.

For as long as we know, men and women have united in some kind of permanent arrangement. According to the custom or law of their community they have mated, produced children and reared them. In almost all instances, the functions of the man and the woman have been clearly understood by both of them. Usually the man has been the protector and the provider of the family; the woman has been his helpmate, and the bearer and nurse of their children.

The functions of male and female were not hit upon accidentally. With his greater muscular strength and power the man naturally took the role of hunter and, later, of tiller of the soil. Given the capacity to bear and nurse children, the woman naturally remained at home to care for her young while her mate foraged for food for them all. Historians now believe that agriculture was probably discovered by women.

In most primitive communities a husband jealously guarded his wife against sexual relations with other men and cast her off or killed her if she was unfaithful to him. Again, this attitude was not motivated by whim. It was the natural outgrowth of the discovery that a woman who had intercourse with a male could become pregnant by him and that the man who was her more or less regular mate could then find himself providing for another's offspring.

Whim or not —

[9]

The practise of wife-killing reflects the low value placed upon female life.

The fact that the consequences of intercourse can be more serious for the woman than for the man led to the creation of a double standard of morality. A man who copulated with someone other than his regular mate would not ordinarily have to pay a penalty for his act; she was the one who became pregnant. On the other hand, a woman who had such relations would involve her husband by obliging him to care for children not his own. Thus in earlier times polygamy—a man's taking more than one wife—prevailed. The desire to increase the population also played its part; one man could keep several childbearing machines going at the same time. Whether a husband was monogamous or polygamous depended on numerous factors—the custom of the community, the ratio of women, the economic status of the male, the desire for many children and so on.

There is no reason to believe that primitive man was promiscuous. The higher animals are not. Some mate in pairs for a while, and some species of apes even mate on a permanent basis. There are birds that, year after year, return to the same community with their original mates. In all but the lowest classes of animal life, fishes and reptiles, parents care for the young. In contrast to fish, for example, apes produce but one offspring at a time and infancy endures for a long period. It takes fifteen years for the orang-utan to reach full growth.

Nor does promiscuity exist among the various primitive tribes scattered about the world today. True, it has often been customary in an exaggerated spirit of hospitality to lend wives to honored guests. It is also true that unmarried girls have been deliberately deflowered as a religious rite, by a chieftain exercising a privilege, or in cases where the groom refused his privilege through fear of spilling his bride's hymenal blood. In these customs, however, one finds no suggestion of promiscuity as we understand the term.

Among primitive people, every male was expected to be married at puberty. Unmarried females were equally rare. The man or woman who reached adulthood without having found a permanent mate was despised and ridiculed. In communities where intercourse was forbidden except for the married, marriage was indispensable.

Of course marriage customs varied greatly among different tribes in different parts of the world and in different periods of history. In some places wives were bought, and an extremely poor man might be unable to afford one unless his parents could finance the son's marriage by marrying off a daughter for a good price. In the Solomon and Easter islands, in the Upper Congo, in some of the Gilbert Islands, among tribes of southern Guinea and in other remote areas, the wealthier men monopolized the available supply of wives, leaving the poorer and usually younger men wifeless.

Out of fear that a bridegroom might not be available for a girl or a bride for a son, the future was made as secure as possible by very early betrothals. It was also desirable for parents to sign up a very young girl and establish her marriage for life because in this way they could be assured of her virginity before marriage. There was also the economic factor; parents could buy a six-year-old girl for their son at low cost, while grown girls often fetched higher prices in the market place.

The more one considers the history of marriage and the relationship between men and women, the more one is struck by the fact that the customs were rooted in the practical necessities and conditions of the times. These considerations were not necessarily confined to conditions on earth. Customs were also determined by these ancient peoples' notions of what their god or gods wanted of them. For example, in ancient China, sons were needed to perpetuate ancestor worship. Thus the single man or woman was not fulfilling his obligations and was a disgrace to his family. In fact, if a wife reached her fortieth year without bearing a son, her husband was compelled to take a concubine. In India an unmarried daughter was thought to be evidence of the disfavor of the gods; parents consequently sought to marry off their daughters as early as possible. Virginity was deemed an essential virtue of the bride, so marriages arranged in early childhood were usually consummated as soon as the girl had her first menses.

Mating arrangements also have taken many different forms down through the centuries. Polyandry—the union of one woman with a number of husbands—existed among the ancient Britons, primitive Arabs, American aborigines, Hottentots and the inhabitants of the Canary Islands, India, Tibet and New Zealand. More recently, it has been practiced in some remote areas of India, Ceylon and Tibet, where male births at times greatly outnumbered female births. In some of these polyandrous societies the woman was a wife taken in common by the brothers of a family.

The Bible contains many references to polygamy among the Hebrews. In fact, they continued this practice until the rabbinical synod at Worms prohibited it in the eleventh century. The Mohammedans were permitted as many slave concubines as they could afford. The practice was widespread over the rest of the world and was known on every continent. It is sometimes forgotten that not until the nineteenth century was polygamy specifically forbidden in the United States.

Many reasons for polygamy have been suggested. The ratio of

The Decline of Sex

men and women was not the compelling factor because the practice existed where there were more men than women as well as where women outnumbered men. Perhaps the most important reason was that men were unwilling to remain continent when intercourse with one wife was taboo—when, for example, tribal law forbade coitus with a woman who was menstruating, pregnant or nursing a child. Since many primitive peoples considered animal milk to be excreta, a nursing mother could remain sexually untouchable for five or six years. A lesser factor that impelled men to seek new wives was that primitive women lost their beauty while quite young, so their husbands sought fresh attractions. Another consideration was that until recent times a man's prestige was related to the number of his children. One with many offspring was respected by his contemporaries and considered to have been especially favored by the gods.

Despite the fact that polygamy has been widespread until modern times, monogamy has been the more common way of life. When man discovered that he could obtain food by working the same land over and over, he ceased to roam about, and the monogamous family became the prevalent one. The civilizations of Greece and Rome were essentially monogamous. The custom of one woman for one man was also given impetus by the growth of Christianity.

Between the latter part of the fourth century and the middle of the sixth, the disintegrating Roman Empire was overrun by barbarians. The Vandals swept into northern Africa, the Visigoths went into Spain, the French penetrated Gaul and the land of the Alemanni and Burgundians, the Goths moved into Italy, the Lombards settled about the Po River, and the Saxons and Angles entered England. These nomadic peoples were originally monogamous, and the father was the undisputed head of his family. This tradition, along with the Christian teaching that the sexual relationship be restricted to one man with one woman in a permanent marriage, doubtless set the pattern which exists today in the Western world.

No one type of marriage prevailed everywhere. The wealth of its male head often determined whether the family was monogamous or polygamous. But regardless of the type of marital relationship, one condition could not change: the woman had to obtain from the male the semen to make conception of a child possible, she had to carry the child for approximately nine months, and she alone was equipped to provide nourishment for the newborn infant.

In modern times we have seen a change in one aspect of this human condition. It is now possible to use a formula of cow's milk and vitamins to provide the nutritional requirements essential for the infant's physical well-being. But while we have discovered a substitute for the mother's milk, we have also learned more surely than ever before that there is no substitute for the love and warmth which a mother provides and which every baby craves and needs for his emotional health. Oh yes there is. Even men can provide love + warmth

An experiment in prewar Germany confirmed this point strikingly. A group of newborn infants were placed in a completely antiseptic environment and artificially fed the most advanced scientific formula. They lacked but one thing: personal love. These children developed a shocking variety of psychological ills. Other children born to mothers who disregarded the ordinary rules of sanitation but who nevertheless put their babies to their breasts and held them warmly and affectionately during the feeding were happy and healthy.

The point of all this is that no matter how much things change,

how well educated women become or how free and independent
they make themselves, their role in sex, pregnancy and childbearing is foreordained. It may be possible and even desirable to
change aspects of the relationship between husband and wife, but
the fundamental condition of that relationship, that the woman
carries the baby and cares for it after birth, is established by the
nature of her being.

Doubtless as a result of dependence upon men for long periods
—during pregnancy and childbirth and while women are nursing
their young—the idea of the "inferiority" of women developed.
This idea has been expressed in almost every culture back to earliest times. Even today the condition of women in some Moslem
lands is difficult for the Western mind to comprehend. In these
countries, a husband is permitted several wives, and some men find
it less expensive to buy a new wife than to pay for medical treatment
to keep an existing wife alive. Except among the enlightened,
many Moslem men still will not let a male doctor examine their
wives. Instead, the husband will accompany his wife to the doctor
and serve as an interpreter, relaying his wife's complaints to the
doctor and the doctor's prescription to his wife. Many Moslem
women are still shut up in purdah and seldom leave their homes,
although this condition is changing.

As a general rule, until recently—and still, in the more backward regions—a woman at childbirth was considered unclean. Before her baby was born, she was forced to stay in a hut away from
the main house—a dirty hut unfit for animals. We need not wonder how the Moslem woman has learned to cast down her eyes and
keep silent in the presence of the male.

European women have a considerably higher position, of

course. Yet the degree of freedom possessed by their American sisters continues to amaze them. Except in the most advanced and educated classes, European women still tend to look upon their husbands as their lords and masters. One well-educated American woman, who studied at the Sorbonne and speaks French fluently, went with her husband to a meeting of businessmen in Spain. The Spaniards in the gathering also spoke French, and the meeting was carried on in this language. After perhaps an hour or so of conversation one of the Spaniards turned to the woman and said with a smile, "Do you know how I can tell you are an American?"

She shook her head.

"When men are speaking, you also speak."

The idea that a woman is entitled to participate in a conversation with a group of men is a new one for many Europeans and, in fact, an unthinkable one for most people in the world.

The gradual emancipation of women in the Western world from the economic and social bondage women continue to know elsewhere can be traced to the influence of Christianity. The Christian teaching that a woman has a soul of her own and is an equal being in the sight of God draws uncomprehending stares in the rest of the world. Yet it is this idea of women's equality before God that underlies the progress they have made.

At the same time, Christianity's attitude toward women was conditioned by St. Paul, who said, in the First Epistle to Timothy:

I wish then, that the men pray everywhere, lifting up pure hands, without wrath and contention. In like manner, I wish women to be decently dressed, adorning themselves with modesty and dignity, not with braided hair or gold or pearls or expensive clothing but with good works such as become women professing godliness. Let a woman learn in silence

[16]

with all submissiveness. For I do not allow a woman to teach, or to exercise authority over men: But she is to keep quiet. For Adam was formed first, then Eve. And Adam was not deceived, but the woman was deceived and was in sin. Yet women will be saved by childbearing, if they continue in faith and love and holiness with modesty.

In other words, the traditional Christian position is that the male is first among equals.

While keeping in mind that men and women are different by their very natures, we must also recognize that what constitute the ideals of masculinity and femininity have undergone drastic, even revolutionary changes. Consider the "ideal male" of earlier times. He was first and foremost strong and courageous. He was the best hunter and the best fighter of his tribe. Looking back in history we find that kings and emperors usually established their leadership over their fellow men through prowess—their courage in battle, their ability to strike down with the sword those who contested them.

Only in relatively recent times has it become possible for numbers of men without great physical endowment to achieve notable success in positions of leadership. Outside the fields of literature and the arts, which have always been a special category in human affairs, the man lacking size and physical strength was almost destined to play a secondary role.

This has changed to a considerable extent. It is now possible for the man who is short and thin, who may lack good eyesight and good hearing, to achieve tremendous success through the exercise of mental and psychological skill. A successful scientist need not be a physical giant, and a financier can understand the intricacies of the business world if he weighs one hundred pounds as easily as if he weighs two hundred and fifty. It is true that large corporations still tend to favor for top management positions men who "look like leaders"—those who are taller than average and give the impression of physical strength. But one need only refer to *Who's Who* to realize that the scientists, businessmen, professional leaders, even political leaders, are not necessarily the biggest, strongest or bravest of men. In the place of physical prowess we have substituted mental and social competence. which women share.

It is ironic but true that the individual who a few hundred years ago might have become a leader among men by virtue of his brawn may now be reduced to one of the lower classes. A man who could endure great physical hardship and perform great physical tasks was once the most admired of men, but today the best he may be able to do is to get a job as a longshoreman and hope that a machine does not replace him. He who might have been the right-hand man of a king in the twelfth century is struggling to eke out a living for himself and his family in the twentieth.

Similarly, the flabby little fellow who might have held no loftier a place in life than that of a lowly jester may now be writing television comedies and earning several hundred thousand dollars a year.

The emotional qualities of the "ideal man" have also undergone drastic changes. The young male who in earlier times felt an urge to prove himself, could do it with his bow and arrow or spear. The valiant warrior was the popular hero of his time.

Now we disapprove of killing, except in war, and we have substitutes—boxing contests, football games, bullfights—all involving combat, all watered-down versions of the old battles to the death. But even the boxing champion, the substitute killer, meets with an interesting change. He now enjoys a limited and decreasing prestige in his community. He may still be idolized by the lower classes but he carries little or no weight among the educated. But the successful professional golfer, whose skill is at least half in the realm of psychology and mental concentration, receives from the better educated, more affluent and more articulate members of modern society a greater respect than the boxing champion.

What this adds up to is that to be considered a "true man" the modern male must be something quite different from the "true man" of even a few generations ago. The modern man is expected to modify his tendency for violence and to express himself less in physical terms and more in emotional and mental ones. The influence of society, expressed by the qualities upon which it places great premium and to which it pays the greatest rewards, tends to make men less masculine—in the traditional sense—and encourages them to develop characteristics which have traditionally been considered feminine.

Yet one must proceed warily in attempting to state what is the real nature of men and women. No matter what general statements one makes, exceptions can be found in history and in modern times. For example, there have been societies in which the woman was the undisputed head of the family and the man was regarded with indifference, if not scorn. In some other societies, women were generally believed to be better equipped to perform hard tasks involving sheer muscle power.

In our own culture the evidence of our senses tells us that men are more inclined toward athletics and are better at them than women, that they take more pleasure in games involving rough physical acts. In saying this we must realize of course that some girls are more athletic than some boys, that some women hit a golf ball farther than their husbands, that some can run faster, that some are incomparably better skaters and swimmers than their mates. There also are women who outdrink, outswear and outswagger the average man. But it is universally recognized that they are exceptions.

It is important to understand that when I stress the distinct differences between the sexes, I am not preparing to discuss whether one sex is inferior to the other. Statistical evidence leaves no doubt that in many respects women are superior to men. But even when one says this, one is implicitly acknowledging that they *are* different.

Thousands of myths have been developed over the centuries to support the argument that women are inferior. Some of these myths have a basis in human experience while others are founded only in blind preconceptions of the male. For example, there seems no doubt that by nature, entirely apart from the cultural conditioning, women are more likely than men to express their emotions. On the other hand, it is a mistake to believe that women are therefore more likely to go to pieces under stress. Records of admission to hospitals for emotional disturbances and actual experiences in situations of stress, such as the mass bombing of cities, belie this belief.

But one need not subscribe to the view of women held by men through the centuries in order to deplore the movement to the opposite direction. The Victorian concept of women did immense harm. Men chose to regard a female as a fragile creature who was unable to control her emotions, yet was expected to exercise the most rigorous and unrealistic control over those emotions dealing with sex. The nineteenth-century woman was expected to be something it is not possible for any person to be. It was out of this unrealistic expectation that the stereotype of the "prostitute with the heart of gold" was born. It was a surprise to discover that a woman quick to respond to sexual stimulation was also one who responded emotionally in everyday, real-life situations.

We must strike a realistic balance based on fact and not fancy. Much mental health depends upon our accomplishing this objective. As a practicing psychiatrist, I concur with Lucius F. Cervantes, S.J., professor of sociology at St. Louis University and president of the Rocky Mountain Council on Family Relations, who says in his book, *And God Made Man and Woman*:

> I am convinced that one of the chief reasons for dissatisfaction in marriage is a dissatisfaction with the other sex in general. A source of marital discontent is the inability of partners to appreciate that men and women are completing and not competing, and that men and women have God-given pre-potentials that make them different physically, emotionally, psychologically, and religiously. A male standard can no more be reasonably set up for the female than a female standard can be set up for the male. Although this may seem obvious, it is this very lack of understanding the differences between the sexes that causes so many marriage-bound break-ups and so much unhappiness in marriage—thus affecting children, society, and of course, the individual married partners themselves.

2

WHAT
SEX
REALLY
MEANS

PERHAPS NEVER HAS ONE WORD SO OBSESSED THE WESTERN WORLD
as the word *sex* does today. It is a word we see and hear everywhere. Yet never has a word been used by so many and its meaning been understood by so few.

What does the word *sex* really mean? It means *all* of the things
that distinguish the male from the female. It means not only physical differences but emotional, spiritual and intellectual differences
as well. There are many such differences, built into our very natures, which affect the functions of men and women in their rela-

tionships with the other sex. We are in the process of ignoring or minimizing such differences and therefore ignoring or minimizing the basic differences in the responsibilities of men and women.

We can find hundreds, perhaps thousands, of indications that modern men and women are moving toward similarity. Some of these indications—women smoking, drinking, driving, pursuing professions hitherto considered the exclusive domain of the male —are hardly conclusive, and may even seem trivial, when regarded individually. Yet when one piece of evidence is added to another the effect and the implications are overwhelming.

If you doubt that there has been a virtually complete breakdown of differences between the sexes (apart from the ever-present physical differences and differences of dress) ask yourself this question: What do men do in this modern world which women are not permitted to do? You will find it difficult to supply one example.

There is hardly a job now considered exclusively male. Tending bar, driving a tractor or a steam shovel, wrestling professionally, racing on motorcycles, welding, riveting, preaching in churches— regardless of what used to be the exclusive province of the male, you will now find women engaged in it.

There has always been some overlapping of functions. Women in the past have taken their stand at the barricades and have carried (literally and figuratively) their men on their shoulders. But when they have done so, everyone agreed they were exceptions. When they do so as a regular thing today, however, more and more people ask, "Well, why not?" These people are saying that there should be no clear distinctions—that a father is as well qualified as his wife to diaper a baby, and should do so; that a woman with a higher earning capacity than her husband may go to work every day while he stays home with the children; that he can wash and iron the clothes while she repairs the plumbing as well as the other way around. There is no difference between the sexes in educational opportunities (or often in how they are educated and what they are educated for). There is a decreasing difference in employment opportunities. And the traditional standards about what he does in courtship and marriage, and what she does, have virtually disappeared.

When the four young men who call themselves "the Beatles" arrived on the American scene in 1964, to set off a ground swell of teen-age adulation, a commentator asked, "Who are these Beatles? You look at their faces and hairdos and you think they are women."

It was not immediately clear to the casual observer whether the Beatles were boys assuming some of the traditional physical characteristics of girls or girls assuming the clothing of men. And this neutrality was a strong element in their wide appeal. Surely they were not being mobbed by thousands of screaming youngsters because of their musical talent; any small town could produce a quartet with equal ability. Rather, the Beatles symbolized a characteristic of the times: the trend toward a neutrality of the sexes. Girls could identify themselves with them and so could boys. And the songs they sang were essentially sexless—a further indication that to boys and girls they represented a common meeting ground.

Another example, also trivial yet also revealing: more and more teen-age boys and girls are having their hair cut in identical ways, so that it is increasingly difficult, if not impossible, to tell which sex is which. This trend is most pronounced in England. *The New York Times* (July 23, 1964) reported that British girls are snipping off their hair, while a large number of young men have let theirs grow. The result, it said, is that it is often impossible to tell the difference between the sexes if they wear blue jeans. And they do.

The *Times* reported that the most commonly seen hairdo, worn by both young men and women, consists of a thick lock of hair hanging over the forehead, long sideburns that look like spit curls, and a shaggy shingle effect in the back. Other young men and women wear lionlike hairdos.

In London a middle-aged tourist from Kansas asked a young person for directions to the nearest post office. She addressed the person as "Miss" but it turned out to be a sixteen-year-old boy with long brown hair, a bright pink suit jacket and light trousers. Significantly, when the tourist realized her mistake she was the more embarrassed of the two. Oh dear.

Another interesting indication of the change in roles of the sexes may be seen on golf driving ranges. One might imagine it the duty of fathers to instruct their sons in the art of hitting a golf ball long and straight, but surprisingly often one sees mothers outdriving their husbands and teaching their boys how to do so. Somewhat more extreme but, fortunately, also more rare is the sight of wives instructing their husbands. And the husbands often accept this instruction docilely and without any outward sign of embarrassment.

When Johnny plays football, baseball or basketball on his elementary-school team, it may be Father who goes to the game to cheer him on, but in many communities it is almost an even chance that it will be Mother. She will be cheering fervently from the sidelines—and in many cases telling him exactly how to play the game.

One might say there is a relationship between the degree of masculinity in the women of a nation and the extent to which they have taken to wearing pants. In Latin countries like Italy and Spain, where men are still the unchallenged heads of their families, it is rare to find a native woman in slacks. If one sees a female wearing pants, one can reasonably conclude that she is a tourist from the north or from across the ocean. And in these areas, I have noticed, pants are worn almost always by women who are engaged in the struggle with men for equality or superiority.

Still another slight yet significant symptom was pointed out by a European visitor in the United States. He was amazed at the number of women who were driving cars while their husbands occupied the passenger seat. "Where I come from, that is almost unthinkable," he said. "The person at the driver's seat is the head of the house, and he literally takes responsibility for bringing his family where they want to go."

An indication of the change in the relationship between the sexes can be found in the kinds of marital complaints brought before the criminal and divorce courts. A few generations ago if a beating was administered in the family, one could be certain it was the husband who beat the wife. Wife beaters have greatly declined in number over the years, for which let us be thankful. But there seems to be an increase in the number of women using physical means of dominating their husbands—and in the number of husbands who meekly submit to such treatment.

In a divorce case, for example, a husband complained that his inability to get along with his mother-in-law resulted in his wife's physically pushing him out and then locking him out of his house —a procedure that would have been unthinkable when husbands ruled the roost. In earlier days when wives wished to do away with husbands, they invariably chose the underhanded means that someone in an inferior and passive position could use. The husband-killing wife might dose his coffee or tea with poison so that he would be dead before he could retaliate. Today's wives who can no longer endure their husbands and want to eliminate them quickly are likely to bludgeon them or stab them to death—an act involving aggressive physical effort.

Middle-aged people will recall the furor created in the 1920's when cigarette manufacturers began to publish advertisements showing women with cigarettes in their hands. The cigar manufacturers are now in approximately the same position as those pioneers of cigarette advertising. For example, the General Cigar Corporation has been running full-page advertisements in national magazines: "Should you offer your Aunt Zoe a Tiparillo? If she smokes, why not?" In some sections of New York City, passers-by do not even turn around to look twice when they see a young woman strolling down the street with a cigar clamped between her teeth.

Few sanctuaries remain for the male. Perhaps the last stronghold to which he could go and be certain to find no woman on the premises was the pool hall. Traditionally pool parlors have been the haven of the cigar-smoking and tobacco-chewing male, and spittoons were as much a part of the furnishings as the pool tables. A woman who entered this hall was either the proprietor's wife or a prostitute: no other conclusion was possible. A woman spectator was "bad," and even the most disreputable of women would not be allowed near the pool tables.

Today, not only has the poolroom become respectable, but manufacturers of billiard tables and other equipment have undertaken a spirited campaign to make the game attractive to women. A "cue lounge"—euphemism for pool hall—was recently opened in White Plains, New York. It claims that 40 percent of its players

[27]

So? what.

are women and children. Here is how it describes itself: "Orange and gold wall-to-wall carpeting. Soft background music (classical no less). Billiard tables in pastel colors, blue, tangerine and gold. A bright canteen area. Soda, yes. Alcoholic drinks, no. Comfortable beige and white Baumritter furniture throughout the playing area. Flush to ceiling, fluorescent lighting."

As the editors of *Look* pointed out in their book, *The Decline of the American Male,* women have ceased to play a subservient role —and indeed have come to play an increasingly dominant role—in American society. They cite these statistics:

There are 1,513,000 more women than men in the United States. Eight years ago (in 1950), there were only 601,000 more. . . . The number of women owning securities has increased 35.7 percent in the past four years, rising to 4,455,000. They own 100 billion dollars' worth of stocks alone—about 60 percent of the individually-owned shares of A.T.&T., 55 percent of Du Pont and 54 percent of General Electric. . . . *Fortune* credits them with control over about 60 percent of all consumer purchases. . . . The Gallup poll reports that the wife participates in managing the funds in 71 percent of American households—and in nearly half of those, the husband has completely surrendered the power of the purse.

The changed relationship between the sexes shows up in the dating patterns of the unmarried. Not so long ago the girl waited for the boy to pursue her. The most she could do, in a ladylike fashion, was to place herself where she could be seen in an attractive light and where her availability would suggest itself to a boy whose eye she hoped to catch. For her to call a boy and suggest a date was unthinkable. An indication of how things have changed is the recently published *Seducer's Cookbook*. Older persons might be forgiven for thinking it was designed for men who sought to entice women to their apartments. The book jacket made plain that its advice was intended for women as well.

A man who held a position as a night clerk in a large motel told acquaintances that he had expected to encounter among the guests some young couples whose marital status was doubtful. "What I wasn't prepared for," he said, "was for boys and girls under twenty to come to the desk with little or no luggage, obviously intending to use a room solely for sex purposes—and then for the girl to dig into her purse to pay the bill."

The disappearance of many of the traditional qualities of maleness and femaleness is reflected in our whole modern attitudes toward romance. Elaine Kendall, writing in *Mademoiselle* magazine, February, 1963, made this comment (as condensed by *Reader's Digest*):

Men and women used to fall in love, quarrel, kiss and make up and live happily ever after. Now no one falls in love. Instead, people experience a mutual attraction, sometimes leading to an emotional involvement, which is hardly the same thing. At best it's self-conscious; at worst, joyless. Even the lovers' quarrel has ceased to exist in its original form. Mutual "attractees" do not quarrel. They have hostilities.

As Miss Kendall observes, "Who wants to dress up and go out on a rainy night to meet someone with whom one has a relationship? It would be more appropriate to wait a day and see him in his office."

Among its many other dubious contributions the advertising industry has succeeded in taking much of the romance and mystery out of the relationships between the sexes, and by doing so it has broken down many lines that once separated the sexes. A young man who thumbs through the pages of a popular magazine or listens to commercials on television may be excused if he is something less than enchanted with his friend of the opposite sex and refuses to allow her to bewitch him with her synthetic charms. Does the girl have beautiful, soft hair? Perhaps—but he knows that the color may not be hers. Even the hair may not be hers. He would be deaf and blind not to realize that, judging by the vast sums spent by advertisers of dyes, changing the color of one's hair is one of America's favorite indoor pastimes. Has she beautiful eyes? Again, he may justly suspect that she uses false eyelashes or eye make-up. Has she a beautiful figure? It may be her own—or it may be aided by a well-padded bra or a two-way-stretch girdle. Are her teeth like stars? Or are they held in place by certain denture preparations? She may exude a provocative fragrance on a date, but he is not fooled. He knows she smells sweet only because she uses a certain deodorant and mouthwash. Her skin may be smooth and silky, but he also knows that she has unwanted hair. In fact, at the urging of advertisers, he may even have given her a razor for her birthday.

As justices in divorce courts have testified, the tyrannical husband is rapidly and happily becoming a thing of the past—if he has not already become so. Today's young bride may marry with the intention of serving her husband, but she knows that she need not endure treatment which her grandmother or great-grandmother might have put up with as a matter of course. She knows that if her relationship with her husband becomes too difficult, she can get a job to support herself and possibly even her children.

[30]

Why should she? why he please her?

That a wife need not put up with an overbearing husband—or even one who has annoying habits or minor idiosyncrasies—is believed on all levels of society. Even Roman Catholic wives who believe in marriage for life show a pronounced unwillingness to put up with what they consider unbearable treatment from their husbands—and the husband shows an equal unwillingness to shrug off mannerisms or character defects which a man in earlier times believed he should endure. As a result, the number of persons who appear before marriage courts seeking separation, which frees the partners of the obligation of living with each other, but does not allow them to remarry, has increased markedly.

While the Equal Rights Bill, guaranteeing women the same wages as men for the same work, was only recently enacted into Federal law, the idea of equal rights in marriage and the abolition of double standards has already developed to a greater extent than most people realize. Today one commonly hears wives say that they will be faithful to their husbands as long as their husbands are faithful to them, but that they will "move off the reservation" if they think their husbands are doing likewise.

One of these "equal rights" marriages involves a man and woman who both work for the Federal government. When they married fifteen years ago, she made it plain that she believed in equal rights, and that if her husband thought his masculinity bestowed any extra sexual privileges upon him, she would prove him mistaken.

He is a good-looking, muscular man more than six feet tall—the picture of masculinity. In reality, he has a weak, effeminate strain. He prefers his wife to be the aggressor in all their relationships, while he enjoys taking a more passive role. His official duties require that he travel a great deal, and he has taken advantage of the opportunity to have affairs with many women in different cities. However, he says he derives little sexual pleasure from these contacts. The effect is more psychological, for he has a deep desire to prove his manhood.

She is an attractive woman who makes friends easily and who would have no difficulty in obtaining suitors if she gave them the slightest encouragement. During one of her husband's trips out of town she hired a private detective to report on all his movements. Armed with a report that her husband had stayed at a woman's apartment all night, she told him that she also felt free to have extramarital affairs. Her conduct soon became notorious, but her husband accepted her affairs without protesting too much since he had engaged in them as well. However, in a drunken moment, a colleague referred to his wife as "America's mistress," and he blew up.

A heated argument with his wife ensued. She refused to give ground and said she would not accept a double standard: if he wanted her to remain faithful, he would have to vow to be faithful to her. He made the promise. As an added precaution, she made it her business to accompany him on long trips away from home. It is interesting to note that he now has a deathly fear of being involved with other women and even shies away from casual conversation with them.

"Equality in the bedroom" has become the slogan of the modern wife. Probably since the beginning of time women have to some extent been able to dissuade or discourage their husbands from intercourse when they were not in the mood for it. This power of dissuasion in male-dominated societies doubtless never took an open form but was covert—by feigning illness, by pretending that the period of menstruation was longer than it really was, and so on. In modern times the woman uninterested in her husband's advances may also find herself with a convenient headache or conveniently tired. But more and more wives now consider their positions vis-à-vis their husbands strong enough to say flatly that they do not want intercourse until they are given their way in one matter or another. In the majority of modern marriages, it seems, the sexual act is initiated (usually subtly, sometimes openly) almost as often by the wife as by the husband.

The extent to which things are moving is illustrated by the tale of the American soldier in Japan who met and married a pretty Japanese girl and brought her back to the States. Part of her attractiveness lay in her attitude that her purpose in life was to serve him. When he returned from business each day, she had his robe and slippers laid out and a cocktail and predinner snack ready for him. Each night she carefully shined his shoes.

A few times a week she went to a laundromat where she made friends with several American-born wives. Soon she was telling them all the services she rendered her husband, and they in turn told her that she was stupid to go to such extremes for any man. They told her where they drew the line in serving their husbands and what they expected their husbands to do for them.

A few days later the Japanese girl's husband returned home to find a note on the kitchen table saying that she had gone to a movie with one of her American friends and that he would find a TV dinner in the refrigerator. It was only a matter of time before he found himself washing the dinner dishes every night while she made long phone calls to her new friends. *Oh, no!*

Margaret Mead pointed out that the distribution of roles between the sexes and the generations in the United States has undergone a profound transformation. There is now a greater reliance upon the immediate family unit—the father, mother and children—than has ever been known before. In previous generations there was less emphasis upon this small unit and more upon the larger family (adult brothers, sisters, aunts, uncles, grandparents) and even upon the tribal unit. Consider the implications of this change.

In other times a child was cared for not only by his own mother but also by his aunts, grandmother or grandmothers, by cousins, by older sisters who may themselves have been married. In short, the care of each child was not the individual parents' sole responsibility but was shared to some extent by all the relatives. Often all these relatives lived together or in adjacent houses. One still sees this kind of life in Europe, particularly in the rural sections, and also in immigrant sections of the United States.

In times of emergency—for example, when a mother was ill—there was almost always a woman relative to care for the children. The tradition that children are cared for by women was consequently very strong, and it was rare to see a father taking responsibility for the hour-by-hour needs of his children or performing tasks like making beds, washing clothes, shopping, preparing food or cleaning up after meals.

The trend, in developed countries particularly, is away from such large family units. Instead, there is a concentration of activities within the little family of mother, father and children. The movement of immigrant families out of their ghettoes, where their relatives lived next door or at most a few city blocks away, is one cause behind this trend. Now, instead of having her mother or aunts nearby to help her, a mother may be an hour away from them by automobile. Another reason for this trend is that employment opportunities have widened, so it is now common for men to move hundreds of miles for a better job, and of course they leave their relatives behind.

The experience of one family shows how the influences of society have broken up large units. Three sisters came to New York from Germany around 1910. They married in the United States and settled together in the Yorkville section of New York, then populated largely by German immigrants. The three sisters and their families never lived more than five minutes' walk from each other. They shared their aspirations, joys and sorrows. If one sister was sick, the others took care of her children and her house, fed and did laundry for her husband.

Of eleven sons born to these three sisters, five took jobs as skilled laborers in New York, but of these five, only two lived within walking distance of each other. One of the other six became a salesman and was moved by his company to Boston. Another went to Florida, two to California (two hours away from each other via thruways) and two took factory jobs in the outskirts of New York City. In twenty years there has not been a family reunion in which the members of any one of the three family groups have been brought together.

When any of these men and their wives encounter difficulties, they must look to themselves to solve them. The idea of calling upon relatives to care for their children while the mother is ill or to help them maintain their home or discipline their children does not enter their minds. The nature of their present way of life requires that if they have problems they solve them themselves.

As a result, these men must perform tasks which would be done by women in other times. Is the wife ill or unable to prepare meals for the family? With no sister, cousin or grandmother nearby to help, the father is the only adult available to prepare meals and clean up after them. Is mother so tied down with the care of a baby that she can't do the shopping? Father must do it. Mother has no time both to wash clothes and to make sure that the children get to bed on time. Again, Father must do one or the other.

We are witnessing the consequence: the large-scale domestication of the male. Indeed, it is now being said that a man, no less than a woman, is not prepared for marriage unless he can do a little cooking, can shop, do housework and care for children.

At the same time, however, the modern housewife is becoming more of a mechanic than anything else. She no longer enjoys the creative feminine satisfaction of making a dress for her daughter, a shirt for her husband, trousers for her son. She has been persuaded that it is better to run to the store and serve as the family's purchasing agent rather than make these things herself. If she spent three hours preparing a meal, making fresh that which could be bought almost ready to eat, her friends would regard her as an eccentric. Distributors of processed foods not only tell the housewife how much time is saved by opening a can and heating the contents, but they mount million-dollar campaigns to disseminate the falsehood that factory-made preparations are tastier than those conscientiously prepared at home.

Manufacturers have taken over housework to such an extent that many young wives have never squeezed an orange, never hulled a pea or a lima bean, never sliced or cut a string bean. Some young housewives have never even bought potatoes with skins on; the kind they use have already been processed and frozen. There are housewives who have never brewed a cup of coffee; they know only how to boil water and then add a teaspoonful of instant coffee.

A mother who wishes to engage in the most creative function of motherhood, the teaching of her children, is often told by the experts to keep her hands off. An elementary school principal recently told a group of parents of kindergartners, "If you try to teach your child reading or arithmetic, you will do more harm than good." Her explanation was that new methods of teaching these subjects had been developed and that parents who taught their children in the old way would only teach something that would have to be unlearned.

The proliferation of so-called experts has left many mothers confused about how they should fulfill their responsibility to take care of their children and prepare them for life. Consider the matter of disciplining the child. Almost every newspaper and magazine contains advice about how to do it. Unfortunately, the advice is often conflicting. Some experts are more permissive than the mother would be and some are stricter. Some with different religious and cultural backgrounds may express viewpoints she has not been exposed to before. Even if they do not convince her that her way of doing things is wrong, they can create great uncertainty in her mind. After exposure to so many different ideas by so many experts, many a mother is utterly confused. Her desire to do a good job in bringing up her children is frustrated, and she comes to believe that she lacks the background and capability to do it properly. She therefore leaves the job to the "experts."

Sex education is a perfect example. Almost everyone agrees that the best way for a child to learn about sex is from his own parents in his own home. With that much said, many experts next imply that parents do not know how to teach properly, neglect aspects of the teaching or fall down on the job entirely. Then they advocate that the school take over the task. A typical mother does not know the correct names for the various sex organs and does not know exactly how the reproductive processes work. When she compares her lack of knowledge with the calm, assured competence of one who has studied the subject at great length, she concludes that she is not qualified to teach her child and that the schools are better equipped to do the job. Another creative aspect of her motherhood is taken from her.

Still another defeminizing influence is the unpopularity of breast feeding, which is now out of fashion, but not because formulas are better or even more convenient. The real objection to breast feeding, I suspect, is that it is too natural, and in the process of "civilizing" ourselves we have come to look upon the natural functions of our bodies with a certain amount of distaste. Physicians are the product of their time and they hesitate to recommend breast feeding, which they know is unfashionable. Yet it cannot be denied that the mother who does not engage in this natural function of her sex is somewhat less of a woman.

The number of impotent males seems to be increasing, at least judging by all the evidence available. Admittedly, this is difficult to prove. In earlier times the impotent husband was not discussed. No wife would have thought of complaining about it; indeed, many a wife was probably happy when this condition existed. Taught to believe that a woman's function was merely to give in to her husband upon demand and to derive no pleasure from coitus, she may have thought that his unwillingness to perform the act relieved her of an unpleasant task. The impotent male may even have been praised for his "thoughtfulness" and "consideration."

Be that as it may, I have observed in recent years a great increase in reported cases of male impotence. Maybe this is due to the fact that the modern wife, who realizes she is entitled to enjoy sex, feels she is being deprived when there is not a reasonable amount of intercourse. She is more likely than she would have been a few generations ago to call attention to her husband's lack of interest in sex. Still, granting that in previous generations impotence may have existed to the same extent but remained hidden, there is also strong evidence that it results from the male's resistance to the greater domination of his life by his wife.

The hen-pecked husband is a likely candidate for impotence. His wife nags so persistently that he withdraws into passivity, yearning for nothing so much as peace, quiet and as few contacts with her as possible. In this frame of mind he is not disposed to initiate love-making. In fact he is inclined to turn it down even if she proposes it.

Not long ago one of the stern-minded, no-nonsense, "I get what I want" breed of women came to me. She said her husband needed psychiatric help because he no longer displayed any interest in sex. He was a fine figure of a man in his late thirties—six feet tall, broad-shouldered, big-muscled, the picture of healthful manhood —the sort of person who, according to the popular conception, would be capable of satisfying any woman. He had not had intercourse with his wife for almost a year, and she had no reason to suspect that he had been unfaithful.

Seeing the two together, I soon realized what was behind the man's impotence. His wife—a tall, thin, thin-lipped woman with a determined jaw—took the initiative in the conversation, held it all the time and would not let her husband add a word. When she referred to him it was in terms of contempt and disparagement. When talking about mutual possessions she referred to them as "my home" and "my car." In private the man confessed that his sister had urged him to give his wife "a sock in the nose" but that he felt helpless in coping with his spouse. So he reacted as the dominated party in marriages usually reacts—by withdrawal. The sexual union was the only aspect of the marriage which the wife could not dominate, and her failure to achieve absolute domination was the cause of her frustration.

That the failure to achieve a satisfactory emotional relationship lies at the root of much male impotence in marriage is proved by the numerous cases of men who are incapable of intercourse with their wives but lack inhibitions with other women. Often the man whose own wife continually belittles him flies into the arms of a woman who will tell him how great he is and make him believe he is fulfilling his masculine role as he dominates the sexual relationship. For this reason, prostitutes feign admiration for the masculine prowess of their customers.

It is almost always wrong to picture the "other woman" as a siren luring a husband away from his lawful wife. In most cases, the husband who seeks sexual satisfaction away from home has, for one reason or another, failed to obtain it from his wife.

A satisfying relationship between the sexes is a delicately balanced one. If the male does not feel he is taking the initiative and is in effect the conqueror, his instinct rebels at the act. He must be the penetrator, and the woman must be penetrated. This simple biological fact makes the male the active participant and the woman the passive one.

Of course extremes in this relationship can and should be avoided. The barbarian male was the complete aggressor; he took what he saw without displaying any concern for the sensitivities of the woman he was taking. We have come a long way since then, and today's male who seeks to conquer does so by kindness, flattery and consideration, so that he has an acquiescent partner, not one who must be taken by force. This is as things should be: there is agreement by both persons concerned, but control and initiative still rest largely with the male. We have tempered the raw conditions of biology with the humane recognition that woman is not just an object to satisfy male passion, but also the possessor of emotional and physical needs which should be satisfied.

We cannot move to the other extreme, with the female of the species traveling about, singly or in packs, ravishing any males that cross her path, for such a condition does not accord with nature. Obviously the modern liberated female does not engage in cave man sex practices, regardless of how dominant a personality she may have.

But there is no doubt that in the psychological realm she often seeks to play the dominant, aggressive role. It is out of keeping with the character of a woman who is aggressive in business or a profession, who spends her days telling men what to do, to return home at night and play the role of the weak, passive member in the sexual relationship. It can almost be stated as a rule that the more efficient, dominant and aggressive the female, the less likely it is that she will be able to achieve a permanent, mutually satisfying sexual relationship with a man. By her own nature she cannot be the submissive one, and the male rejects the role of submission.

The modern preoccupation with position in intercourse offers some insights into the changed relationship of the sexes. It has been traditional for the woman to adopt the bottom position while the man lies above her bracing his body on his knees and elbows. In such a position the woman is his prisoner hemmed in and unable to break loose.

The emancipated woman is delighted to discover that the traditional position is not the only one. It is possible to lie side by side, in a position that symbolizes partnership, rather than the subjection of the female.

But one sees increasing indications that a favored position among women is one which puts her on top of the male. Now she is in control, at least symbolically. It is she more than he who is responsible for the union of genitals. Women who prefer this position advance many reasons. Some say it is more comfortable. Others, whose religious scruples keep them from using contraceptives, say that in this position the likelihood of conception is reduced (a valid point). Some say their husbands prefer it this way. Whatever her reason, however, a woman who adopts this position is rarely, if ever, a weak, submissive, traditionally feminine type. In most cases she dominates her marriage in other areas of life as well.

A wife who insists that this position is the only comfortable one should not be surprised if her husband displays less interest in her. A woman told a psychiatrist that her husband had become impotent and had been unable to have intercourse for almost a year. The husband, it turned out, was financially dependent upon her. She inherited a family business, operated it and hired him to help her run it. But she made all the major decisions and reminded him that he was continually dependent upon her and would be nothing without her. In bed, naturally, she continued to express her dominance. His indifference to her sexually was his only way of asserting his own individuality. He found himself completely unable to be the passive, complacent and acted-upon member in the sexual relationship.

This impotence he directed only against his wife. Without her knowledge he often visited a branch of the business and spent some time there with a young typist upon whom he could express his maleness. Far from being impotent with this young woman, he had relations with her three or four times a week.

Is it not paradoxical to decry the disappearance of differences between the sexes at a time when evidence of sexuality is pounding in upon us from all sides? Evidence of sex, primarily in terms of the sexual act, is everywhere. In the modern world one would have to be both blind and deaf to avoid daily contact with sex enticement. In the words of Dr. Clark Vincent, chief of the social sciences section of the National Institute of Mental Health: "Ours is a society which condones, contrives and consumes sex enticement. The current notion that sex is fun openly permeates our novels, films and plays. It is the keynote in the way we sell many of our products and services, and the beauty queen is the centerpiece for everything from football games to trade."

This seeming contradiction can be explained easily. The physical differences between the sexes are about the only major differences that remain. The innate desire to find differences and the deep feeling of men and women that there must be differences accentuate this last remaining difference out of proportion.

Never in history have man and woman been so continually and emphatically reminded of the fact that he has a penis and she has a vagina. The preoccupation with sexual intercourse is so great that it may almost be termed an obsession. Nowhere is this more apparent than in those modern novels that describe how to wring the last bit of physical pleasure out of the act. The modern novelist sees the relationship between a man and woman as nothing more than the meeting of different bodies. Literature is a reflection of life. As reflected in our novels sex is no longer an emotional and spiritual act between persons with distinct personalities. Often all that concern the novelist are the explicit physical acts the male performs on the female and she performs on him. And once orgasm is reached, the act is finished, with no greater significance for either party, no more lasting effect upon their personalities, than the sharing of a meal. Even less, perhaps—since the eating of a meal together is less of a physical act, there is a greater possibility of knowing and appreciating the different personalities.

Many popular marriage manuals also betray this fixation on the physical. Almost completely absent is the understanding that in intercourse there is an emotional and spiritual meeting as well as a physical one. There are prolonged discussions of the parts of the partner's body to caress and stimulate, and the positions in which to place the organs for the greatest physical effectiveness. True, one should understand the physical nature of intercourse to enjoy it on a physical level. But the greatest and most lasting satisfaction, which many writers of marriage manuals overlook, comes from spiritual and emotional communion—the communion of two *different* personalities.

3

THE
BATTLE
OF
THE
SEXES

IN A SEEMINGLY ENDLESS NUMBER OF CASES THE STRUGGLE FOR
power between modern husband and wife begins after they leave the
church or the office of the justice of the peace and continues relent-
lessly day after day until the marriage is dissolved by death or
divorce. The source of this power struggle is usually the fact that
the modern man lacks any clear idea of how much control he
should exercise in marriage (many think he should exercise no
control at all), while the modern woman often thinks she knows
more about everything that matters than does the man who married her.

Consider the case of Mr. and Mrs. E, who were thought by friends and relatives to be an ideal couple. He is a biologist with a high-paying job in the research laboratories of a large pharmaceutical firm. She is in the last stages of study for a doctorate in American government, which she expects to use as a college professor. They have been married six years, are childless and have no intention of becoming parents as it would interfere with her career. They live in a fine apartment, well furnished and well stocked with excellent wines, of which she is a connoisseur. To an outsider, Mr. and Mrs. E have it made. They are bright, physically attractive, poised, alert, sophisticated. Those who talk with them for even a short time invariably come away with ideas on current events which had not occurred to them before.

Inside the home, however, and visible only to perceptive outsiders, an unremitting battle for power is being fought in daily conflicts over who should handle the family income, who should decide how to spend their leisure time, who should perform chores around the house and so on. What hardly anyone knows is that Mrs. E has had several luncheon appointments with her husband and her husband's immediate superior, at which she has made it a point to check up on how well her husband is doing at his job.

Nor do many know that when a serious question arises over money or other matters, Mr. E consults his mother and follows the advice she gives him. His mother is also a dominating woman and she considers it natural for women to make the major decisions about the running of a house and the relationship between husband and wife.

As might be expected, Mr. E is a wretched individual who feels completely trapped. He has taken to drowning his frustrations in alcohol, and battles over his drinking have become frequent.

Where this marriage will end is still unclear, but from the direction in which it is moving, one can be certain that more trouble is in prospect.

Next consider the case of Mr. and Mrs. A. It differs from many others only in that five minutes after meeting them anyone will conclude that here is a dominating woman who would not be satisfied with a saint for a husband. Mr. A is the personnel director of a corporation and supervises a department of twenty-five persons. He has written extensively on personnel problems, is considered an authority in his field and is highly regarded by his professional colleagues. Yet if one were to take the wife's word for it, he is an oaf who must be told when to go to bed and when to get up, how many drinks to have before dinner, even how much butter to put on his bread. To total strangers she recounts examples of how helpless her husband would be without her by his side to tell him what to do.

Somehow this marriage has limped along for twenty years. During this time it was customary for Mr. A to travel to many of his firm's factories and branch offices across the country, and on such trips his wife always accompanied him. One summer she became seriously ill. Her doctor told her she should spend several months recuperating and that trips with her husband were inadvisable. So Mr. A went alone to the West Coast.

When he returned, he told Mrs. A he had met an interesting woman, also an expert in personnel relations, and that they had many professional ideas in common. Their discussions had taken place at cocktail parties to which both had been invited and once at lunch with this woman alone. There was no marital infidelity or anything close to it. In fact, the husband commented that this woman was older than he and had an unattractive face and figure.

Despite the harmless nature of this friendship, Mrs. A objected to her husband's conduct and to his enthusiasm when telling her of this woman. Her pride would not tolerate his finding another woman interesting, even in a strictly professional way. She accused him of harboring a secret passion for the woman. Thereafter she turned a cold shoulder to him whenever he tried to have intercourse with her.

Here is a case of a wife with a dominating character and abnormal pride. She displays hostility to all sex, and her life seems to be devoted to taking a sadistic joy in proving that men are inferior to women not only morally but in everyday affairs as well.

Many marriages begin with the implicit understanding that the wife will be the dominant partner. It is now customary for the prospective bride and bridegroom to agree that she will continue to work after marriage and at least until she is well along in pregnancy. Rare indeed is the modern wife who, like the bride of a few generations ago, goes directly from her honeymoon into the role of full-time housewife. Even when a husband can easily support his wife, she usually wants to keep her job. Note that the determination that a bride should work after marriage is generally made by the woman herself, not by her husband.

A marriage counselor who gives instruction classes to engaged men and women used to suggest that wives become full-time housewives as soon as they were married and let their husbands become the sole providers. "I've seldom had such resistance to any idea I've ever proposed," he reported, "and most of this resistance came from the women themselves. I thought that I was speaking on the brides' behalf, trying to relieve them of a responsibility. But they don't mind the responsibility because of the feeling of independence that goes along with it. One woman summed up the feeling of many of her sisters when she said, 'I don't want to have to ask my husband for a cent.' "

Many husbands and wives make a good adjustment if the woman continues to produce some income, provided she does not earn more than he does. Once this happens (and it is happening more often) not only is she independent of her husband but soon he may even depend upon her for luxuries he could not buy himself. The relationship then undergoes a significant change. What wife can resist thinking that her husband had better behave himself if he wants her to continue to support him? She can hardly avoid the conclusion that her own standard of living would be more comfortable if she did not have a husband to support partially.

Ego is a fragile thing. Once a husband begins to think that he is not being fulfilled as a male and is occupying an inferior position in the marriage, he is likely to look for evidence that his wife is trying to lord it over him. He may fight back by trying to become so dictatorial that she will lose her idea about who is the new head of the house. But if she resists his efforts to dominate her, he may retreat from the contest. He may become indifferent to her sexually, look for other partners who will not make him feel inferior or use alcohol to soothe his battered ego.

It strikes me as an increasingly dangerous practice for a boy and girl to marry with the understanding that she will work to support him while he continues his education. When he permits this he mortgages any sense of accomplishment in what he will achieve. His wife may not come out and say so directly later on (maybe she will), but such an arrangement implies that he could not achieve success without her help.

His own sense of self-reliance is minimized. He denies himself the satisfaction of overcoming obstacles and reaching an objective by his own powers. It may be true that behind every so-called self-made man there stands a woman, but it is a rare man who wants to admit this fact—even to himself. If a woman must stand behind her man, his sense of masculinity is protected only if she stands far enough behind him that no one will doubt that he is the doer of the pair.

There also seems to be a greater than usual risk of marital disharmony when husband and wife work together in some joint enterprise, such as a business they own. One reason for this may be that in most partnerships one person almost invariably becomes the boss, to the dissatisfaction of the other. However, if such a joint enterprise does succeed, I imagine it causes less discord than when the wife works independently. In the latter case the husband is often jealous of her success in her field, whereas they can take joint credit for anything they achieve working together.

It is well known that when a husband and wife disagree over money matters, a struggle for domination is going on. Frances Lomas Feldman commented in her book, *The Family in a Money World:*

> Money is used in a variety of ways by both marital partners to exacerbate marital discord. One partner often uses his own ingrained habits of spending as a means of attacking the other. For example, a husband may be controlling about money, holding his wife rigidly to a tight budget or doling out an "allowance" to her. Actually, this may be a role expectation, culturally determined. He may come from a home in which his father, like others in his social circle, was the authoritative, thrifty provider. Such controlled disbursement of money, on

the other hand, may stem from the husband's recollections of hunger and deprivation in his youth.

To certain neurotic husbands, money may be an unconscious symbol of masculinity and power. The wife's retaliation against his money behavior may take several forms. She may spend money wastefully as a way of expressing hostility toward him or as a means of maintaining a dominant role. She may make no effort to operate within the budget he has prescribed, or she may respond by setting limits of her own in meeting his sexual, physical or psychological needs. She may even bring charges against him of inadequate support.

If a wife objects to her husband's spending money on after-work drinks with the people in his office, she is saying in effect that she does not have enough to spend on herself or that there are other things the money could better be spent on. The wife who runs up a big charge account against her husband's wishes is saying that she intends to do as she pleases regardless of how he feels about it—in other words, that he is not going to boss her around.

In every marriage since the beginning of time there has been a struggle for power. In every durable marriage common meeting ground must be found, a compromise between absolute domination by either the husband or the wife. Even in societies in which the husband holds a position of unquestioned dominance, a wife can use many wiles to weaken his influence or to get what she wants from him, while she still maintains the fiction that her lord and master is in full control.

Today money and its control can affect marital harmony more than they ever have. We live in a materialistic society; to a greater extent than ever before the pleasures we derive from life are bought pleasures. Our society takes it for granted that happiness consists in the things we use. The woman who owns an automatic dishwasher is automatically happier than one who washes dishes by hand. The family with two bathrooms tiled from floor to ceiling is naturally happier than one that takes turns in the morning to use an untiled bathroom. In other words, the good life consists of the things we can buy for ourselves or our children.

The advertising industry can accept the major credit for developing this philosophy. This billion-dollar industry is basically devoted to making people dissatisfied with their present possessions and way of life, so dissatisfied that they will get rid of their two-year-old automobile, refrigerator, television set or other possession and buy something up-to-date. If we are a materialistic people who have lost the ability to find pleasure in the simple (and free) things of life, we can thank the advertising industry for making us so.

Because money and material possessions play such a big part in our lives, control of the family income is a more significant factor in marriage than ever before. The one who decides whether to spend the disposable income on this year's car or that piece of furniture, this summer vacation or that addition to the house, is the one who decides how the family will achieve its happiness or unhappiness, as the case may be. To a greater extent than ever, therefore, the person who controls the purse strings dominates the marriage.

Women are coming more and more to control the way the family income is spent. Once again, we can thank businessmen for their contribution to making this so. Every major manufacturer of a consumer product designs and advertises it to appeal primarily to the woman of the house. Were she not inclined to insist that her own taste prevail, the vast influence of the advertising fraternity would not exert most of its efforts to making sure *she* selects the product.

In the purchase of automobiles, for example, manufacturers have found that the woman is intrigued and impressed by the color schemes, the wall-to-wall carpeting, the interior and exterior finish and the many other features that have no effect on the safe or efficient functioning of the vehicle. Most cars are sold in the United States on the woman's appraisal of its styling; it is not unusual for the family not to know whether there are six or eight cylinders under the hood.

To exploit this increasing decision making by wives, some automobile salesmen have taken a lesson from the more progressive coffin display houses and have hidden microphones about the showroom. While a husband and wife think they are discussing things in secret, a salesman at a distance is listening to every word. He easily discovers which model appeals most to the woman and which features are most to her liking. He can then emphasize the qualities she favors and answer any objections she has. The husband could just as well have stayed home, except that by being there he gives the woman a chance to let the salesman know her real attitudes.

An almost endless array of statistics can be cited to prove how American wives have taken control in this area of the marital relationship. The General Federation of Women's Clubs recently reported that 85 cents out of every dollar spent by the family is handed out by the wife. What is more, she often stands behind her husband as he spends his 15 cents, telling him what to spend it on. Equally significant is a finding by the Institute of Life Insurance that well over half of the checks written on joint bank accounts held by husbands and wives are written by the women.

[53]

In addition to gradually taking control of the purse strings, modern wives attempt to demonstrate superiority over their husbands in other ways. An attractive college-educated woman married a high school dropout who worked in a supermarket. After two years they were on the verge of divorce. When they went to a marriage counselor on the advice of their clergyman, the wife kept using the biggest words she knew. Often her husband did not know what she was talking about, and the counselor had to tell him what his own wife had been saying. It was as though the man and woman spoke different languages and needed an interpreter. In a private session with the counselor the husband said that in his presence his wife always talked that way with better-educated persons. The wife denied that she was trying to embarrass her husband. Yet it was obvious to any outsider that she acted like a parent spelling out words before a child.

What brought the couple to the counselor was the husband's unwillingness to have sexual relations with his wife. This was one of the few ways he could strike back. The wife apparently did not object because she was being denied physical satisfaction. It annoyed her that her husband was expressing a negative opinion regarding her desirability.

Another woman, thirty-nine years old, had been married twelve years and had had eight miscarriages but no children. She admitted that she wanted to dominate her husband, but she also gave strong evidence that she neither loved him nor wanted any children by him. There were indications that her many miscarriages were due to psychosomatic disturbances. Subconsciously she realized that if she took on the responsibility of motherhood she could not remain independent of her husband.

Another woman was engaged in a seemingly lifelong struggle to dominate her husband, without much success. She had constant thoughts that if he died she would be on her own again, with a substantial annual income from his estate, which she could spend as she pleased. She did not want children either, but she became pregnant nevertheless. She has dominated this child, a boy, for all of his fifteen years and has taken out all of her aggressive feelings on him. During his childhood his mother handled him with extreme brutality. A physical examination revealed scars on his head and body, where she had hit him with sharp objects and belt buckles. Once she cut him with a knife and on another occasion broke his arm. The physical assaults stopped when he reached adolescence and could defend himself, but she expressed her rejection in worse ways—by criticizing him constantly, telling him how inadequate he was and refusing him the usual freedoms accorded youngsters of his age. Because of his mother's treatment of him and because his father did not know or care about what was going on most of the time, the boy became a teen-age delinquent. His antisocial behavior is easily explained by his wish to escape the family environment and his apparent conclusion that even being sent to a reformatory was better than living with his mother.

The increasing domination of husbands by wives is not confined to any income level. Sometimes it is even more pronounced in the higher levels than in lower ones, where the wife may hold a job and be economically independent of her husband. Walking through a neighborhood with new homes in the $50,000 range, I discovered a striking indication of the change in roles. The kitchens were in the front of these houses and had large windows which enabled passers-by to see what went on inside. After the dinner hour the casual stroller could see an almost shocking number of men in the kitchen preparing the dishes for the dishwasher—presumably while the lady of the house was in the living room enjoying her after-dinner smoke.

Incidentally, a widely published magazine advertisement for electric kitchen equipment pictures the father, with a frilly apron tied around his waist, placing dishes in the family's new dishwasher while the mother and child wave good-bye as they depart through the open doorway. The implication is that that family is happiest in which Dad does such chores most cheerfully.

The demands made on their executives and junior executives by big business and big government almost make it natural for wives to be the dominant figures in the home. The typical executive must spend so much time attending to the details of his job that he is glad to have the management of his home and the making of basic decisions affecting his family's life taken out of his hands.

As a rule the corporation executive works longer hours than the ordinary employee, often in monklike dedication, in order to keep abreast of developments in his company and in his industry in general. Even if he spends only thirty-five hours a week in his office, he must spend lunch hours thinking and talking about business matters, often give up Saturdays and Sundays to business travel or business-related recreation with present or prospective customers, and night after night take home a briefcaseful of papers and publications to read.

Of course large corporations are aware that their successful executives lack time to function effectively in the business world and to be heads of their homes as well. This is why so many corporations will not hire a man for an important job without looking into his home life to make sure his wife can manage matters without him.

Printer's Ink reported in August, 1962: "Although most companies don't publicize the extremes to which they sometimes have wife analysis, few will consider a man for an important position without first appraising the woman behind him. At one large company, roughly 20 percent of its otherwise promotable employees are passed by just because of their wives."

And what is it that employers want to know about the woman at home? The personnel executive of one giant corporation confided: "What we want is a wife who won't be a drag or worry to her husband. We don't want a wife with a drinking problem. We don't want one who greets her husband at night with a list of complaints about the children, the neighbors or the repairman—or with any other problems she can't handle by herself.

"We don't want a wife whose husband has to worry that she may be running around with other men while he's at the office or out of town on business. We don't want one who asks him to spend time running to Boy Scout or PTA meetings.

"To put it bluntly, what we want is a wife who lets her husband come home when he's ready to come and doesn't bother him about a thing."

What this corporation is looking for in its executives can be stated in other words: It wants a man who is the number-one boarder in his home, someone who is entirely free of the responsibility of marriage and of making the basic decisions for his family; a man who lives only for his work, who saves his energies for the office and has all the major decisions and problems of family life made for him.

Under the pressure of the feminization of men and masculinization of women, many men are losing one of their most precious traditional possessions—the right to be alone occasionally and to do as they please with their own time. This is a natural development. The modern mother, particularly in the suburbs, thinks she is not doing her job unless she supervises her children from the time they awaken until they go to sleep. She constantly checks up on their games, making sure her children "relate well" to other youngsters, stepping in if the games become rough and there is the slightest possibility of injury, however trivial, warning them against running too fast or playing too hard because she does not want them to become tired. Such a mother seems to have an uncontrollable desire to run people's lives. So it is perhaps natural that she will try to run her husband's life as well. It hurts her if her husband wants to do something on his own, without her help or guidance.

I visited a young couple in their thirties who had just bought a home near Washington, D.C. Like most new houses this one needed much work before it really could be called livable. Showing me through the house, the wife pointed to a small, dark, windowless corner of the basement. "Eventually," she said, "here's where we'll put Tom's workshop. But before we do that I want him to plant shrubs around the front and sides of the house. Then he has to build a walk between the front and back doors so the children won't be tramping mud over my good carpet. And then I want him to build a fence to keep the children from running into the street."

"What does Tom intend to use the workshop for?" I asked.

"Well, first I want him to build some shelves for the children's room so we'll have a place to keep their books and toys," she said.

"Then I want him to build tables and benches so we can eat outdoors in warm weather."

"And after that?"

"I haven't decided yet," she said.

She never seemed to realize that Tom might be entitled to decide for himself how to spend his spare time. As far as she was concerned, he was supposed to do what he was told. Incidentally, this wife is an ardent advocate of equal rights for women. She does not realize that she already has more than her share of rights and that she should give a few to her husband.

The deterioration of the American father's influence is often flagrantly revealed when his daughter gets married. It is a rare father who is consulted about his daughter's wedding plans. Of course, in a well-adjusted home, the father may be present when such plans are discussed, but it is soon evident that his opinions about the major decisions—whom to invite, where to hold the reception, what kind of service and ceremony to have—are never sought. If he dares to offer opinions, they are completely ignored. It is the mother's and daughter's show all the way—and if he demands an equal say, they will probably be outraged at his poaching on their territory. The bills for the wedding? That is an entirely different matter. It is his duty to pay without a whimper.

Only one other thing is generally expected of him—that he be dressed properly when he escorts his daughter up the aisle. Before and after that duty the ideal modern father makes himself as inconspicuous as possible. Preferably, he retires to a room where he can write the checks without bothering the other members of the family.

When there is but one child and the father and mother are engaged in a struggle to dominate the family, the youngster becomes one of the spoils of war. The father and mother vie for his favor in order to win his support against the other. His good will becomes a prize, and his ill will is a punishment to be avoided at almost any cost.

The result is that the child rules the roost. Mother cannot do enough for him when she is with him, and neither can Father. Let her decide he needs disciplining for some reason or should be denied something he wants. Father, seeing an opportunity to show that he cares for the child, insists (in front of the offspring, of course) that the child should get what he asks for. In this way, Father feels, he is gaining a point in the popularity contest. Or let Father decide that the child must do something—go to bed, stop watching a television program and do his homework, perform some chores around the house—and Mother finds a way to undermine his authority. The child quickly learns to play one parent off against another; by giving or withholding affection he can get anything he wants.

The parents in such homes would agree in one thing at least—in denying that they are giving their child the worst possible training for life and marriage. They tell themselves that they are doing everything for the child, giving him all the advantages they themselves lacked. But they are really making him the most underprivileged of children, for they are denying him training in self-discipline, in learning how to say "No" to impulses. They are keeping him from the realization that he cannot have his own way all the time and that successful living consists in often making one's own desires secondary to those of other people.

Some of the most disturbing examples of the child's being used as a pawn in the struggle between his parents exist where husband and wife are divorced and one parent has custody and the other has the right to visit the child at stated times. In one case a judge awarded custody of a girl to the mother but said that the father could have his daughter for a week end each month. From the moment the father picked little Joan up, on the first Saturday of each month, he could not do enough for her. Anything she wanted —entertainment, clothing, food—was hers for the asking. He usually took her to a toy store and bought her the most expensive items in stock. If she wanted to stay up till midnight watching television, that was all right with Daddy. What he wished to avoid at all costs was his little Joanie's frown or even the slightest indication that she preferred her mother to him.

When the father returned her on Sunday night, the mother knew she was in for a difficult week at least. Whenever she asked Joan to do anything—to pick up towels she dropped on the floor, to set the table for dinner, to help clean her room—the little girl drew her mouth tight and remarked that Daddy didn't make her do things like that. By the time the mother managed to get her to obey the ordinary rules of family living, Father arrived to begin spoiling her all over again.

The mother was understandably bitter about this arrangement. But the main reason for her bitterness is significant. An objective observer would say that little Joan was receiving incredibly poor training for life. She was learning to get her own way in everything and was using her affection as a tool to pry out of others what she wanted for herself. It is not difficult to visualize this girl as a wife, using sex to force her husband to give in to her any time a serious difference of opinion arises. The mother recognized this and complained that Joan's father was undermining her efforts to teach the child the basic principles of getting along with other people. But the mother's major complaint was that he was trying to "buy" the child's affection, thereby making it more difficult for the mother to hold it. In other words, she was most concerned not about what the father was doing to the child but about what he was doing to her.

One can state it as a general rule that when parents consider their own popularity with the child more important than his development as a person, and when they shrink from disciplining him because they fear a loss of stature in his eyes, they are not doing their duty as parents.

One concomitant of the struggle between the sexes is all to the good, however: the male has been made aware that his wife has as much right to enjoy coitus as he has. Much of the credit for this development must go to the authors of the various marriage manuals, which have become as much a part of the modern bride's wedding equipment as her bridal veil. These manuals stress the importance to both wives and husbands of physical caresses and the whole variety of activities which come under the heading of love play. Today, as a result, it is the rare male who considers his wife something of a harlot because she takes pleasure from his extensive caresses or seeks to prolong the love-making as much as possible.

But if it is true that wives in the past were kept ignorant of the pleasures of sex, it may be equally true that today's brides are overly aware of them. In fact, the modern girl often makes her acquaintance with them when she begins to date, and religious leaders complain that they cannot convince adolescent boys and girls that they have no right to petting and other forms of sex stimulation. Many a modern girl has as many orgasms behind her when she marries as her grandmother had at the menopause.

While the emancipation of women has liberated them sexually, it has tended to inhibit some men. The coldness or seeming impotence of husbands is sometimes almost the only outward sign of their resentment at losing control over their marriage.

From childhood boys are taught to mask their feelings. On the one hand, they must not cry if they are hurt physically or emotionally; "Only sissies do that." On the other hand, they must not vent their feelings of rage or anger; this is not "nice." The young man who seeks a place in the business or professional world must adopt a mask of pleasantness. He may hate his boss, detest the customers with whom he deals, find some business associates repulsive. The rules of employment require that he affect a pleasant smile and pretend that all's well with the world.

A man who has been conditioned through life to hide his true feelings will doubtless find it difficult to express himself fully in marriage. If he harbors resentments against his wife, denied a normal outlet for them he will lose interest in her as a mate. And the wife, thinking all is well with her marriage because her husband does not fight with her or contest her will in family decisions, cannot understand why the relationship in bed is so unsatisfactory.

One young man began his marriage by turning over his weekly salary to his wife and allowing her to write all the checks for rent, utilities, phone bills and the other items involved in running their home. Each week she gave him a certain amount for his personal expenses. This arrangement worked for a time, but then he found he needed more each week to cover lunches, cigarettes, cocktails and other incidentals. His wife refused to increase his allowance by the amount he sought because she said the money was needed to furnish their home. Thereafter, there were prolonged arguments whenever he had to ask for additional sums for items like office parties and presents for co-workers who were to be married. He now seems complacent when it is necessary to discuss his financial needs with her—but he finds it impossible to work up any enthusiasm for her as a sexual partner.

4

THE
CLOUDED
MIRROR

IF THE MORE ARTICULATE MEMBERS OF SOCIETY MAKE ANY COM-
plaint about woman's role in the modern world, it is likely to be
that she does not take an active enough part in business and the
professions. Paul Foley, vice-chairman of the McCann-Erickson
advertising agency, in the March, 1964, issue of the *Atlantic
Monthly,* lamented that only two of the United States Senators,
eleven of the 435 Representatives, and four of the 427 judges were
women. He deplored the fact that so many American girls rush into
marriage during their late teens or early twenties. Compelling ar-

guments can be advanced against teen-age marriage, but what Mr. Foley obviously objects to is that women are adopting marriage as their lifetime work. For example, he claims that men are "developing a real respect" for women who choose to remain unmarried—a statement which can hardly be substantiated.

What is most annoying to those who agitate for the expanded participation of women in business, the professions and government is that they meet the greatest resistance from the women themselves. For example, Dr. George Gallup has found that a greater prejudice exists against a qualified woman presidential candidate than against a qualified Jew—and this prejudice is greater among women than among men. In fact, only 51 percent of the women polled would vote for a woman presidential candidate.

Even well-educated women prefer, in the main, to expend their energies as wives and mothers rather than in careers. In a paper delivered before a symposium on the potential of women sponsored by the University of California, psychologist Eleanor Macoby of Stanford University reported on what has happened during the thirty or forty years that large numbers of women had been able to obtain higher education on an equal basis with men.

A Madame Curie is conspicuous by her rarity. Even in the field of letters we have more men than women who are productive, creative writers. When it comes to achievement in science, the imbalance is much greater. Our colleges produce very few women who become intellectually excited by, or immersed in, a scientific problem; or who organize large bodies of diverse data into a new theoretical statement (*The Nation,* March 23, 1963).

As I commented, it annoys the feminists to be confronted with the reality that the majority of women continue to be most interested in having children and in living happy lives as wives and mothers. For example, Betty Friedan is notably upset in print over most women's lack of interest in issues she thinks should interest them. She decries the amount of space the women's magazines devote to subjects of purely feminine interest, such as the care and feeding of children, the ways to please a husband and how to make more attractive meals.

In *The Feminine Mystique* Miss Friedan asserts that these magazines ignore the real needs of the American housewife. What she overlooks, however, is that of all the classifications in magazine publishing, the periodicals devoted to "women's interests" are by far the most competitive. They are now engaged, and have been engaged for years, in a frantic race to attract readers. Their editors try to publish material that will appeal not to the relatively few who endorse Miss Friedan's book but to seven or eight million women every month. And these editors have become convinced by readership surveys and their own experience that children, husbands and homes are the subjects of greatest appeal to America's women.

Miss Friedan quotes a social psychologist who showed her

some sad statistics which seemed to prove unmistakably that American women under 35 are not interested in politics. "They may have the vote, but they don't dream about running for office," she told me. "If you write a political piece, they won't read it. You have to translate it into issues they can understand, romance, pregnancy, nursing, home-furnishing, clothes. Run an article on economy or the race question, civil rights, and you'd think that women never heard of them."

But Miss Friedan does not give up easily. In her view there is something like a conspiracy with the goal of "denying women careers or any commitment outside the home." The conspirators, of course, are men. She writes that on most of the women's magazines of which she disapproves, the deciding vote is cast by men. Women edit the housewife's service department, but what they edit is the product of men's minds, she says. Despite Miss Friedan, however, the cold truth remains: every month some thirty million women read the major women's magazines, and there is no evidence that these women are forced to buy the publications they read so avidly.

The feminists also overlook the fact that men can marry whom they choose, and that men do not want to marry women who are filled with the good solid qualities—dependability, intelligence, ability to manage a household and so on—and nothing more. Often such women are unmarried and without prospects for marriage. The reason? They lack the one thing that would make them appealing—the qualities of womanliness. These qualities do not consist only of a pretty face and figure—what we have come to call sexiness. They run deeper. They are the qualities that make a man feel he is a unique member of the partnership, and that the woman, in her uniqueness, is a complementary member. A national magazine—a woman's magazine, no less!—put a sharp point on this idea when it ran an article entitled "It Takes a Woman to Make a Wife."

It may well be true that there are more unhappy housewives today than at any time in the past, but this proves little. It may be equally true that there are more unhappy husbands, more unhappy children, more unhappy older people. Moreover, it has been my experience that the married woman who embarks on a career outside the home is as likely to develop emotional problems as the one who remains at home. This is not to say that many women with intelligence and ambition are not better off pursuing careers; it is only to say that many women with full-time jobs might well be better off if they went back to their kitchens. When we deal with individuals, we must be careful to avoid blanket judgments.

For instance, it would be quite wrong to argue that all career women are maladjusted simply because Miss R is. Yet many cases like hers could be cited if one wished to make a general point.

A thirty-eight-year-old woman in Washington, Miss R fits most perfectly the ideal of the emancipated career woman. She holds a responsible position as the head of a section in one of the departments of the Federal government, where she supervises the work of hundreds of men and women. At her desk she is crisp and dynamic, and her male subordinates admire her efficient, decisive way of doing things. Her competence is more marked because her predecessor was a weak, hesitant man who feared to make even routine decisions without clearing them with his superiors.

This woman is tall, physically attractive; she dresses well and is well educated; she comes from a fine family. In a city like Washington, where social graces are important in a wife, she would be an asset to any man. She knows how to entertain graciously and manages to appear poised under almost any circumstances.

Good looks, breeding, education, manners—superficially she has everything. But she is unmarried. Her only male friends are a few section heads, her equals, with whom she has an occasional lunch or dinner. She has never had a serious relationship with a man. Nor is it likely that she ever will have. For she is temperamentally equipped to resist any man's efforts to subdue her in the bedroom.

This woman, who carries herself in such a refined way, takes a vicarious pleasure in reading obscene books and magazines. She has a collection of photographs showing men and women in the most perverse heterosexual and homosexual acts. Ironically, her friends and acquaintances are extremely circumspect in her presence. They are afraid of shocking her if they use even mild profanity or discuss the normal, ordinary facts of sex in her presence.

Is she unhappy about her condition? Of course. Is she typical? Of course not. She probably would have had problems if she were married, a mother and a housewife.

The nature of the times we live in is such that almost everyone is subjected to pressures which tend to make him insecure, less certain of himself and his place in society, and consequently more susceptible to doubts, fears and worries. Over all of us hangs the threat of atomic war—a war which could erase in an instant all our plans for our own futures and those of our families. There is also the lesser but nonetheless ever-present possibility of sudden accidental death. At the pace at which we live—with our faster and faster means of transportation, for instance—a sudden accident on the highways or in the air may snuff out life immediately. Probably no one ten years old or older does not know of at least one person who has died suddenly in an accident.

Emotional uncertainties that arise from modern living are even greater. A few generations ago a child had a fairly clear picture of his life as an adult. In all likelihood he would do the same kind of work as his father or his uncle. He would marry the kind of girl his father married, one with the same religious belief and from the same cultural background. As a parent he would face virtually the same problems his parents faced. Even if he sought a different way of living, he would find that society had built-in devices to make change difficult.

In this century there has been a revolution in our way of living and in our morality. The vast changes which have taken place and which continue to take place make it difficult or impossible to learn from the experiences of the past how to deal with the present, much less the future.

A few statistics reveal strikingly that in our complicated society, everyone, not just the housewife, is a victim of tension. In the United States more than a billion dollars is spent each year on hard liquor alone, and most of the 216 million gallons consumed annually is used to relieve the symptoms of underlying anxiety. About $245,000,000 worth of tranquilizers is consumed in the United States every year, along with $172,000,000 in sleeping pills. Tension is an occupational hazard in business; where you find a group of successful businessmen, you also find a high percentage of ulcers and other psychosomatic disorders. Social critics who speak of the unhappy modern woman might consider the possibility that her husband is unhappier.

The rationale for the campaign to get housewives out of the home is the idea of many feminists that the "happy housewife" is a myth and that, by and large, the woman who stays at home minding the house and caring for her children inwardly resents her lot. There is no denying that many wives are unhappy about the lives they lead. But so are many husbands and many children. The times we live in are difficult for everyone.

This is not to say that many a well-educated woman who considers herself trapped at home, talking only to the diaper man, the milkman and the clerk in the supermarket, is not deeply desirous of making a greater, more tangible use of the education she has received. Nor do I mean to imply that some women with genuine talents—perhaps the artistically gifted, those with highly developed instincts for helping others, those who are potentially brilliant writers—may not be stultified by the traditional *kinder-kirche-küchen* environment. For their own fulfillment such women may need interests outside the home. A Phi Beta Kappa who has majored in journalism and developed an interest in political problems will probably not be satisfied scrubbing floors and washing diapers.

If such were the kind of woman to whom the feminists refer, it would be difficult to disagree with them. But the fundamental question is this: How many wives and mothers actually feel a need to become intellectually or emotionally involved in matters outside their own home, family and local community? Unless one denies all the evidence presented to the senses, one must conclude that most wives and mothers are more interested in fighting for a traffic light at a dangerous school crossing than they are, say, in raising the agricultural potential of the undeveloped nations of the world.

Let me add that this statement is not intended to be just another man's indirect way of implying that the male is superior. All of us—male and female—are more interested in our own local problems than we are in those of the nation or the world.

It would be foolish to give a few off-hand reasons why the unhappy housewife is unhappy. If we know anything about this problem, it is that every individual has her own aspirations and interests, and that these are blocked in a great variety of ways.

The unsupported generalization about unhappy housewives circulated by Miss Friedan and others may have the effect of the self-fulfilling prophecy, however. If you tell a person often enough that he will do something terrible, he may eventually believe it himself and do it. Then you can claim you were right all along, disregarding the fact that you put the idea in his head in the first place. Similarly, if you tell the mother of small children that she *should* be unhappy staying at home with them, she may begin to question her own happiness and then come to believe that she is miserable.

Miss Friedan has achieved this effect. Not long ago the Class of 1944 of Smith College held its twentieth reunion. The theme of its meeting was the book written by Miss Friedan, who is also a Smith alumna, Class of '42. One woman commented: "Raising the issue has caused much unnecessary unhappiness and dissatisfaction among women who were perfectly content."

According to a report published by *The New York Times,* "the majority of alumna attending the reunion proclaimed their satisfaction and lack of frustration with being full-time housewives and part-time community volunteers." These women, it must be remembered, are graduates of one of the most prestigious women's colleges in the country. They would be expected, if anybody would be, to be discontented with the role of wife and mother. If a majority of Smith alumna find satisfaction in being wives and mothers and nothing more, it seems reasonable to assume that this job will be even more satisfying to women who have not had such a fine education and who are content with a less challenging intellectual environment.

As a rule the woman who insists most vehemently that members of her sex have as much capacity for intellectual and business achievement as men and should take an equal place in the competitive world is one who is herself highly intelligent, well educated and ambitious to realize her potentialities in roles other than those of childbearing and homemaking. After all, most women who have access to a public platform are in this category. Therefore, on this subject we hear from only a small segment of women, who are truly not typical.

The feminist reasoning is something like this: "I am educated, intelligent, competent. I can perform a service for society as well as many men and perhaps better than most. It would be a crime to discriminate against me and to deprive me of the opportunity to use my talents in a constructive way for the good of society simply because I am a woman."

So far so good. But now the error creeps in. "I happen to be a woman, and therefore what is true of me is true of all women. I would be miserable if I had to confine myself to the home, to something no more stimulating than a daily exchange of conversation with the diaper man or milkman, and if I had to devote my life to serving a man who might be my intellectual inferior. I am a woman, and I feel this way. Therefore other women feel this way."

Her mistake is in thinking that most women have the intellectual aspirations she has and that most of them feel themselves deprived and even imprisoned, as she would if she had to live their kind of life. We are told that in his sex life an upper-class white American has more in common with an upper-class Asiatic than with a lower-class American. A similar comparison can be made about the case of the educated, ambitious woman. She has many things in common with the educated, ambitious man that she does not share with the typical woman, whose aspirations run in an entirely different direction. To put the matter bluntly, the highly articulate, well-educated woman is not a true spokeswoman for womanhood in general. She speaks out of her own unique experience and for only a small part of the female population. What she says may be perfectly true for herself and others like her, but it is hardly true for all her sisters. In fact, she does not even speak the same language as most women.

The past erred in saying that because most women should be in the home, and in fact prefer to be there, to bear and teach children, and comfort and give emotional support to their husbands, all women should be this way. If you examine the suffragette movement closely and discount the extreme statements of over-ardent feminists, you will see that it was a reaction to the tradition that exiled all women to the home and allowed none to exercise talents and abilities that were unusual or exceptional. Unfortunately, extremism is a vice that humans find hard to control. In saying that it is cruel to confine a gifted woman to the nursery and kitchen for life, many people go to the opposite pole and argue that the typical woman, who is happy to play the traditional role of wife and mother, is an involuntary prisoner, the victim of insidious male-originated propaganda. This is simply untrue.

5

WHAT EVER HAPPENED TO FATHER?

FROM THE MOUTHS OF CHILDREN COME SOME OF THE MOST RE-
vealing insights into the way the sexes are losing their traditional
identifying characteristics. A young child of troubled parents often
gives extremely bizarre answers when asked whether mothers or fathers are likely to perform certain acts. A five-year-old girl said that
mothers smoke but that daddies do not; that daddies pay the bills
in restaurants but that mothers give them the money beforehand;
that daddies are always "nice" and that mothers are the ones who
spank children when they are bad; that when the family is going

someplace, it is mothers who decide where to go and who make sure that daddies and children are ready in time; and that whenever there is trouble between Mommy and Daddy, Mommy always tells Daddy how bad he is. This child's answers make it clear that she pictures her mother as the dominant figure in her family.

The effect of this child's picture of the family on her future actions cannot be exaggerated. To a great extent we are all actors, playing a part in life. The world's a stage and men and women merely players: we take the role expected of us. The girl who gets the idea that her function as wife and mother will be to boss her husband, dominate her family and discipline her children will try hard to play that role. If her husband, with a different idea of her function, tries to prevent her from playing the part she has in mind, she will have many difficult moments before she reconciles the conflict between what she envisions as her role and what her husband conceives it to be.

Mental pictures about fathers and mothers that are directly at variance with the traditional images are probably found most often among children whose parents have both worked outside the home and who have been cared for by professional caretakers, relatives or friends. In a typical case a mother worked as a teacher and she was either teaching, attending graduate school or marking test papers from seven in the morning until eleven at night. She was the sort of person who pours all her energy into one thing at a time, and for her, motherhood was distinctly of secondary interest. Her husband worked from nine to five and actually saw much more of his son than the mother did. The boy was cared for by the husband's father, a retired widower, during the day. Now the lad is eight years old. In his own home he sees that caring for children is a task for men, while mothers earn the livelihood, or at least a major share of it. Of course he sees that in other families the father works most of the time and the mother cares for the children. This conflict between life as it is lived in his own home and life elsewhere has given him a murky picture of what he should do when he grows up and threatens to become an unsettling influence in his life.

Once he asked his mother why she had to work so much. He wanted her to stay home and take him to a picnic sponsored by the school PTA. "How did you think we've been able to buy such a nice car and nice clothing?" she asked. "We have these nice things because I went out and earned the money to buy them."

This mother plays the role of the enlightened modern woman. She denounces the "Philistines of the market place" and looks down on businessmen and others whose primary interest is to make money. Yet she is implanting the most materialistic ideas in her child's mind. She is telling him in effect that material possessions are worth more to a person than parental care and attention. The child, as a consequence, sometimes makes bitter remarks. "I wish I had a mother and daddy like other people," he once commented.

In my practice I see many cases in which the lack of a father's strong masculine influence has had a noticeable bad effect on his child's development. Sometimes these children talk freely for hours about their home life, their school, their recreation, how they spend their vacations and holidays, and throughout all this conversation and discussion the word "father" is never mentioned. There may be some recognition of his existence, working in the background to provide the family income, but he never becomes more than a distant figure who makes no impression upon the child in terms of personality, example or discipline. Life goes on the same way whether the father is at home or not. Sometimes he is away from home so often on business trips and spends so many week ends and evenings with business associates that his child could be excused for failing to recognize him when he sees him.

Not long ago such a father—a vice-president in a big advertising agency—suffered a heart attack at his desk, was rushed to a nearby hospital and died within an hour. His twelve-year-old son was called home from school, and his mother explained what had happened. The boy stood silent for a moment, then asked, "Does this mean we'll have to sell our Cadillac?"

Shockingly large numbers of children know no more than the general kind of work their fathers engage in. Nor is this ignorance confined to young children. Even college students often have no more than the sketchiest idea about their fathers' work.

A college junior, under treatment for emotional disturbance, was asked, "What does your father do?"

"He's the sales manager for the X company [a corporation with branch offices around the world]."

"What does he do?"

"Oh, he's in charge of sales."

"Does he supervise the work of salesmen? Is he also in charge of advertising? Is he responsible for sales of all the products the company makes or just a few?

"He's sales manager—that's all I know."

A few more questions revealed that the young man had never been in his father's office, had never discussed the responsibilities of his position, did not know how many employees he supervised, could not specify any of the decisions his father had to make.

Is such a young man atypical? I doubt it. I have observed that young people of every age and social position know less about the responsibilities and day-to-day problems of their fathers than preceding generations did.

A partial reason for this ignorance is that the growth of big corporations and big government has made the employee's individual contribution less important. The modern worker has less of a sense of accomplishment than the worker in a small factory or business who sees the direct result of his actions. Moreover, fathers in other times worked closer to home, often only a short walk away, and the children could see at first hand exactly what their father had to do in order to make a living. Suburban children often live an hour or more from the father's place of business, they do not see it in the ordinary course of events, and when they could do so, on week ends or holidays, the office is closed. All the details pertaining to his employment are obscure and misty in their minds.

Even fathers who try to fulfill their traditional role in the family often find it difficult to give their children a clear understanding of the work they do. One reason they fail is that much of the modern world's work, on the administrative level at least, goes on inside a person's brain. If you watch a professional or businessman at work—a lawyer, doctor, accountant, labor leader—you usually will see very little physical action. Since an observer cannot tell what they are thinking, it is difficult for him to grasp clearly what their jobs entail. This is also becoming true in automated industries, where a worker who is continually watching dials and other indicators to make certain that all the machines are functioning properly seems nevertheless to be just sitting at a desk doing nothing.

Contrast this with the typical nineteenth-century worker. What he did was physical; it could be seen. Often without saying a word he could instruct his son in his techniques of earning a living.

But today's sons find it difficult to imitate their fathers, for they do not see anything they can imitate. In a great number of cases all they know is that their father works with his brains, but they are unable to identify themselves with his work in any way. A cartoon in *The New Yorker* magazine summed up this situation: It pictured a small child saying, "I don't know what my father does, but it makes him sick to his stomach."

It should follow that children lack respect for what their father works for—namely, the money he brings home each week or month. How can they respect the value of a dollar if they do not understand how much effort he must exert in order to earn it?

In earlier times, the child who saw the amount of effort involved in raising and cooking food could easily understand why it should not be wasted and why everything on one's plate should be eaten. Today? School garbage pails after any lunch period are filled with perfectly edible food which the children have decided not to eat: sandwiches bitten into once and then discarded; fruit that has been tossed away without having been touched; even unopened lunch bags thrown away because the little ones decided they would rather have ice cream bars.

A visitor from India spent a few days in an American home and looked on with disbelief and dismay as a child told his mother to cook two eggs for breakfast and then proceeded to eat less than one of them. "I can't stand cold eggs," the child protested. In his own country the Indian knew people who get less to eat every day than this American child discarded after each meal. He said he almost wept openly at the sight of such waste.

Not unusual was the reaction of a fifteen-year-old boy who had ridden his bicycle to a playground and then had been given a ride home in a friend's car, forgetting about his bicycle. When he returned to the playground, it was gone. His father roundly berated the boy for losing the bicycle. The lad later expressed astonishment that his father had been so annoyed. "After all, what does it matter to him?" he asked his mother. "All he has to do is to take ten seconds to write a check for a new one."

A twenty-two-year-old girl, a college senior, began planning in March for the graduation present she expected from her parents in June. She informed them that many classmates were receiving three-month trips to Europe, and she let it be known that she expected equal treatment. When she was told that her father had already gone into debt to finance her education and that the family could not afford such a lavish present, she accused her parents of "putting on the poor mouth" and lying. She refused to talk to them for several weeks. Her parents became so distressed at her anger that the father took out another personal loan to give her the trip she wanted. Even then she was not entirely mollified. In a candid moment with her mother she said, "If it was that easy to get the money, I can't understand why you and Daddy were so difficult about it."

The lack of identification with their fathers' occupations has bad effects on boys particularly. As I mentioned, in order to achieve the full potentiality of his masculinity a boy identifies himself with the dominant person in his home. Traditionally, of course, that dominant figure has been the father. Not only was he the final arbiter and judgment maker, but he also had the responsibility of seeing that decisions he or his wife made were carried out. When he spoke, his word was respected as law by both his wife and children. Moreover, he lived much more closely with his family. He was a fine example of what masculinity is all about, a model for a boy to follow. The boy, seeing his father act as the dominant member of his family, prepared himself to be the dominant one in his own family when he grew up. Thus from his father he learned how to act when he himself married and fathered a family.

We have a terrifying example of how the absence of strong fathers and husbands can affect the mental, physical and social health of a people. The example is the American Negro. As many authorities have pointed out, the Negro male taken from his home in Africa and reduced to slavery underwent an experience similar to the destruction of human personality wrought in the Nazi concentration camps. Charles E. Silberman, in *Crisis in Black and White,* describes the development of the system which was designed to deprive the American Negro man of all sense of masculine identity and which has destroyed ambition, prevented independence and eroded intelligence for the past 350 years. Silberman writes:

> In this newly-developing capitalist society, the laws of slavery have developed with a blinding logic and simplicity; slavery became an absolute and total condition in which the proprietor owned the slave's mind and soul as well as his body and labor. Because there was no precedent for slavery, the jurists of the new colonies had to find precedents where they could—in the laws governing chattel property. A horse, a cow, a house, have no rights vis-à-vis the owner. Thus it was with this new type of property. . . .

[83]

More important, the slave could not enter into a contract
for any purpose since "neither his word nor his bond has any
standing in law." Hence a slave could not marry: slaves could
live together but their relationship had no legal status. . . .
Slave law not only refused to recognize marriage, it reversed
the common law tradition that children derive their status
from their father, maintaining that "the father of a slave is
unknown to our law." To have held otherwise would have
raised the embarrassing question of what to do with the numerous children born of a white father and a slave mother; the
old common law would thus have created a large class of free
mulattoes. Thus a slave father not only was legally unknown,
he was legally stripped of the last semblance of masculinity,
his right to his marriage bed. . . . In general, therefore,
what sexual contact there was between slaves was bound to be
casual and temporary.

The systematic destruction of the Negro male's position as the
head of his family and the leading force in his family's life continues in the present. For instance, it is easier for a Negro woman to
obtain employment. She can almost always find a job as a houseworker or maid, doing work that white women are reluctant to do.
Even at a time of general unemployment, when Negro men are out
of work, there is a continuing need for Negro women as domestics.
So Negro women have grown accustomed to being the chief providers of their families and by virtue of this fact have become the
most vital force in Negro family life.

An appalling picture of what life is like in a society where life
without father is the rule rather than the exception was given by
William Longgood in the *New York World-Telegram and Sun* in a
description of the Fort Greene Housing Development in Brooklyn.

What Ever Happened to Father?

In this project, there are 3,455 families, 63 percent of them Negroes, and 25 percent Puerto Ricans.

But a more significant statistic is that 75 percent of the Negro families are broken [he wrote]. In almost every case, this means a woman living alone with children.

For the new male tenant, it's like moving into a harem. Having a man is a status symbol among the women. The problem is so acute, the competition so brisk, that the maintenance men are warned not to let themselves be beguiled into bedrooms.

The question is bigger and more far-reaching than abstract morality. It is fundamentally economics. Rents must be paid. Unattached women get lonely. So they resolve both their problems at once by throwing what are called rent parties.

A rent party provides women, alcohol, narcotics and numbers—all at a price, of course. The parties usually take place Friday night, pay night. On Friday night it's like Paris, according to one description. The place lights up. There are fights, beatings, shrill music, hammering on doors and pounding on walls, wild screams, a perfect bedlam.

Saturday morning, the place looks as if it was hit by a hurricane. And then Saturday night is a repeat performance on a more modest payday scale.

This housing development, according to this report, is a place of violence: fights, wife-beatings, assaults, rapes, stabbings, gang battles, even murder.

For the young at Fort Greene, sexual promiscuity comes early. It is the only free recreation available. Many girls are said to be pregnant by the time they are 14 or 15. They are likely to have five or six children by the time they are 23 and are getting funds from Aid to Dependent Children. A girl may be introduced to sex by her mother, who sells her at a rent party.

In the race riots that rocked Negro communities in the northern United States in recent years, it is significant that the main rioters were teen-age boys who have lived their lives without family examples of responsible manhood to serve as models for them. These youngsters drift aimlessly and have no way of knowing what is expected of them as responsible, mature men, husbands and fathers. The only men that many of these youngsters can observe at close range are the unemployed, who spend their days on street corners. These children have never had the normal experience of living in a home where the father goes to work every day, is the family wage earner and accepts his responsibility as the head of the house.

Note that this pattern of life and the absence of a strong father go together. Puerto Ricans, who have a different cultural background, rarely get involved in the rent parties; they are more likely to band together and stick with their families. There are only 14 percent of broken families among them, compared to the 75 percent for the Negro families.

Although the delinquency statistics of Puerto Ricans in the United States are lower than those of Negroes, they are considerably higher than those in Puerto Rico itself. This condition is traceable to the fact that in Puerto Rico the father is without doubt the dominant figure in the family and that boys therefore have strong male figures to emulate. Even in the poorest parts of the island the father is usually the major and often the only wage earner, while the mother stays home to care for the children.

What Ever Happened to Father?

When Puerto Ricans migrate to the United States, however, the women often find it easier to get jobs—as houseworkers, as sewers in the garment trade, as restaurant help, for Puerto Ricans and Negroes face the same employment problems. So the Puerto Rican father in the United States is often no longer the major support for his family. He may even be unemployable, while his wife can earn a wage. Meanwhile, his children are learning the American conception of a good father: the man who gives his family a well-built, fully equipped home in a good neighborhood, a new car every two years or so, and other material comforts. They note that their own father is unable to provide these things, and consequently he ceases to be the influential and powerful person he was back home where less emphasis is put on material possessions. Add to this state of affairs the fact that many Americans consider the person who cannot speak English an inferior, no matter what his other attainments. Thus you have the makings of a sharp decline in the father's influence—and of a consequent increase in juvenile delinquency.

But it is a gross mistake to think that juvenile delinquency is confined to Negroes, Puerto Ricans and other members of the underprivileged classes. Newspaper stories reveal characteristic disturbances among the middle and upper classes: discovery of narcotics rings among the children of well-to-do parents in many suburbs of New York City; the admission of a high school student in Connecticut that "it's not a party without a bottle of booze and at least the chance of having intercourse"; the widespread destruction wrought in such places as Daytona Beach, Florida, and Hampton Beach, New Hampshire, by youngsters with enough money to travel hundreds of miles and take long week-end vacations; the grim story, repeated over and over, of serious, often fatal, automobile accidents involving young drinking drivers; the increasing numbers of teenagers with no real need who break into homes "just for the thrill of it."

The common pattern behind the delinquent behavior of these young people with the greatest material comfort ever known is that they have been deprived of the same thing as their brothers and sisters in the slums—the presence of a man they can look up to and imitate. These delinquent boys and girls from the suburbs are usually the children of professional people, business executives, social, civic and political leaders. Yet they seldom see their fathers and rarely communicate with them. For the fathers are so busy working to provide material comforts that they have little time left to provide spiritual and emotional ones. One boy who burglarized a home and stole jewelry for which he had absolutely no need summed up this distortion of values. He was rebuked by his father, who had had to bail him out at the police station. "How could you do such a thing?" the father asked. "You didn't need this stuff. Your mother and I gave you a car and all the spending money you could use—a bigger allowance than anybody in your class. We gave you everything. And now you pull a stunt like this."

The son lifted his head and looked his father in the eye. "Yes, you gave me everything," he said. "But the thing that you didn't give me was the thing that you valued most—your own time and thoughts. When you gave me the car and the allowance, you were just buying off your guilty conscience. You would rather give me a hundred dollars anytime than spend a few hours in my company."

In Britain as in the United States the authority of the father has been gradually deteriorating. The British mother in increasing numbers now goes out to work. In many cases she earns nearly as much as her husband, and she is no longer content to be the docile helpmate. Because Dad's prestige in the family has declined, his youngsters find it possible to play off their mother against him. This helps explain the increase in teen-age brawls which have spread across the British Isles like a plague.

Ever since World War II and the emergence of woman from the home, bands of teen-age hoodlums and vandals have caused trouble in England. There were the Elephant Boys, from the notorious Elephant and Castle slum section in southeast London, who roamed about the city just after World War II. Then came the Teddy Boys with their tight pants and swinging watch chains. More recently, there have been the Mods, who effect a dress that is almost feminine, and the Rockers, who drive motorcycles and wear leather jackets, boots and helmets. When Mods and Rockers come into contact, trouble is spawned.

The story is told in grim statistics. In 1938, the last full year before World War II, only 11 boys in every thousand between the ages of fourteen and fifteen were indicted for juvenile crime in Britain. By 1962, less than twenty-five years later, the rate had more than doubled, to 26 boys per thousand. More shocking still, the rate of juvenile crime trebled among girls.

As Roul Tunley observes in his world report on juvenile delinquency, *Kids, Crime, and Chaos,* in almost every country in the world it is recognized that the father is a key factor in preventing juvenile delinquency.

In Germany, the well-known juvenile court judge in Freiburg, Wolf Middendorff, said, "A boy learns to be a man by copying his father. If there's nothing worth copying, the boy soon senses it and turns to other heroes."

In Japan, before World War II the father was a little

emperor, with absolute rule in his own home, just as there was a big emperor with absolute rule at the head of the country. There was little delinquency. But the system was feudal in nature and doomed to failure sooner or later in the modern age. "Unfortunately, we haven't had time to work out a satisfactory substitute for this system, which is why we have such a delinquency problem," said Haruo Abe, Japan's public prosecutor.

In Turkey, which has not yet felt the real upheaval of modern progress and where delinquency is low, or at least hidden, the father is still supreme. Mrs. Suheyla Kunt, an attractive Istanbul housewife, who is one of the few people active in child welfare work there, told me that her father selected her husband for her (an arrangement, incidentally, which worked well), and that when she was growing up, she was so fearful of her father's judgment that she never did anything without asking herself what he'd think of it. "When I was a child," she said, "I was only allowed to kiss my father's hand on festival days. This still happens in the small towns and villages, but it's changing in the big cities."

Karl-Erik Granath, of Stockholm's Child Welfare Council, believes that one of the reasons for Sweden's swollen juvenile problem is that with the removal of the family from the country to the city the father's role has diminished in importance and that no adequate other arrangements have yet been worked out.

The lack of a strong father is also characteristic of the family backgrounds of unwed mothers. In her study, *Out of Wedlock,* Leontine Young, professor at the School of Social Administration of Ohio State University, makes this blanket statement:

If one factor can be considered fundamental in the family background of unmarried mothers, it is the consistent pattern of domination of the home by one parent. With monotonous regularity one hears from girl after girl, as she describes her early life, of a family which has been shadowed by the possessiveness and unhealthy tyranny of one of the parents. Rare indeed is the girl who can remember parents who loved and respected each other and who shared family experiences and responsibilities with each other. In a great many cases an unmarried mother comes from a broken home and is brought up literally by one parent only, but in a large number of cases the parents remain together and the effect is much the same. The domination of one parent deprives the girl of normal relationships with either. . . .

The great majority of unmarried mothers come from homes dominated by the mother. The basic pattern is consistent in all of them although it varies in degree. The mother is basically a woman who has never accepted her own femininity and whose life adjustment is a constant struggle with that fact. To a greater or lesser degree she both envies and despises her husband, and she generally marries a passive man who cannot or will not oppose her domination of the family. Possessive of the children in most cases, she has been both seducing and rejecting in her attitude toward them. While much has been written about the damage done by this kind of mother to her son, she can be equally damaging to a daughter.

A typical mother of a girl who became pregnant out of wedlock was a woman I will call Mrs. Y. She was well educated, possessing a master's degree from one of the most highly regarded Eastern universities. She was a successful businesswoman and managed an office with more than a hundred subordinates, both men and women. From the day of her marriage she dominated her husband, even to choosing his clothing and dictating what ties to wear with his shirts. For instance, one evening when she and her husband were getting ready to go to a restaurant with guests, he appeared with a blue shirt and blue tie. While the guests stood by, she instructed him to go upstairs and change to a white shirt. He did so sheepishly, like a little boy.

In her home she made not only all the big decisions but all the little ones as well. In fact, when her twenty-year-old daughter began to undergo psychiatric treatment, the girl found it difficult to recall any time when her father had managed to gain his way over her mother.

The daughter herself had been completely dominated. She had wanted to attend a boarding college, but her mother decided that she would be better off at home under supervision. Whenever she spent an evening with girl friends, Mrs. Y questioned her at length about her activities. Before her infrequent dates, her mother insisted upon seeing her escort and quizzing him about his family background. When the girl returned, she had to undergo a third degree about every activity, with particular reference to any efforts young men might have made to display affection.

Of course supervision is ineffective in the modern world if the girl herself wishes to have intercourse. In this case the girl met a boy she was indifferent to, but she practically forced him to take her to a motel where they spent several hours together. A month or so later she told her mother she was pregnant.

Mrs. Y's first question was "How can you do such a thing to me?" Her basic concern was not her daughter's shame and anxiety, but the reaction of friends and neighbors.

Immediately she set about making plans to conceal her daughter's condition from them. She found a home where the girl could live while expecting the baby, made arrangements to turn the infant over to an adoption agency and even worked out a plan to have picture postcards, written by the girl, mailed from foreign capitals, so friends and neighbors would think she was on a trip abroad. When the daughter said she wanted to keep her baby, the mother answered that she would throw them both into the street.

The deceit worked perfectly. The girl returned home looking none the worse for wear. The mother then set up more stringent safeguards to prevent such an event from recurring. One day, when the girl had presumably gone shopping at a supermarket, she drove out to a country road with a casual acquaintance and became pregnant again.

The mother was outraged. She called her daughter a harlot, and was mystified about why this had happened again. The woman was unable to see the obvious: that there was a direct relationship between the mother's lifelong domination of her daughter and the girl's desire to become pregnant. This was her form of rebellion against a tyrannical mother.

To all these events the father was a mere spectator. And he was astonished when somebody suggested that if he had been a real father, these pregnancies probably would not have happened.

Sometimes a father's absence cannot be avoided. There is bound to be trouble later unless his wife minimizes the disadvantages of his absence by making the children aware of him, by displaying his picture prominently, discussing his activities with them, explaining that he must be away through no choice of his own, reading his letters aloud and making sure that the children communicate with him often, and doing things in a certain way because that is how Daddy would like to have it done. If this is done, he does not come back as a stranger, and he can quickly assume his proper role.

When there is only one effective parent, his or her personality will become dominant in the household. Whoever takes responsibility for the children is likely to overemphasize certain qualities, and if this extremism is not modified by the other parent, the child may become a perfectionist, overly meek or overly brash, too much this way or too much that way. As a rule, men tend to be too dictatorial when they are the sole parent, and mothers tend to demand too little from their children. Either extreme is bad.

While the main reason for the decline of the father is the rise of the dominant mother, strong social influences are also at work. Television programs show Dad as a moron, and the children (almost invariably more sensible than he) take their direction from their mother. Most books on child care are directed at mothers and encourage them to make the major decisions alone. And large business concerns have made it quite plain that they want employees in supervisory or executive positions to put job interests ahead of family interests.

Vance Packard points out in *The Pyramid Climbers* that the people who hire or place an executive like to regard his home as a peaceful haven where he can rest in a worry-free, problemless environment. They are concerned if his wife bothers him with family problems, if she is a free spender or a haphazard bookkeeper—in short, if she burdens him with family responsibilities.

The higher up the ladder a corporation executive moves, the more likely it is that his position in the home will suffer. On the one hand, he must become so devoted to his work that he has little or no time to spare for questions that arise at home. He forces his wife to be the decision maker and encourages her independence— the same masculine qualities he uses in his work. At the same time he becomes accustomed to VIP treatment. The more important his job, the less does he hear the word No from his subordinates. He is likely to have a dedicated secretary who has learned to anticipate his wants. All day long, at his office, at the expensive restaurants where he eats, at the plush hotel where he stays when traveling on an expense account, servants rush about to fulfill his wishes before he expresses them.

It is a rare human being who can throw off the characteristics of the executive, who gets people to do things at his word, and play the role of suitor toward his wife. Everywhere else people do what he wants when he wants them to. Why should he have to spend time on acts of tenderness to produce acquiescence in his wife? Packard quotes an official of a leading management consultant firm who describes the typical executive as "a hell of a poor lover" because "it is hard for him to get through his head that his partner is within her rights in not being in the mood to do what he wants to do."

While the modern corporation wants the wives of its executives to stand on their own feet and not bother their husbands with the trivialities of running a home, they do not want the wife to be too independent. As Packard says, "The company's top officials may worry about the man whose wife has her own career. Will she, in pursuing her own position, neglect her role as the ever-adoring little lady at the fireside? And will her career prevent her from being an asset for the company in community affairs?"

As a result of large corporations' demands of wholehearted devotion from career-minded employees, the father grows aloof from his family. On the rare occasions when he does discipline his children, he tends to be either too lenient or too hard because he is not familiar with all the facts involved. Peter Wyden declares in *Suburbia's Coddled Kids:*

> One difficulty is that most phantom fathers don't become involved in problems of discipline until after the trouble has ripened into something reasonably serious. Then they are summoned to appear before teachers or principals or psychiatrists, usually before the 8:05 train or evenings or Saturdays. Not having known much about the trouble as it grew, the men tend to over-react and over-punish. This heaps a new burden on the mothers who must supervise the serving of whatever sentence of punishment is imposed.

Corporations that investigate the wife before hiring the husband can be badly fooled. A man was being considered for a high executive position with a large corporation in the Washington area, and the person doing the hiring invited the prospect and his wife to dinner. The wife appeared, well groomed, soft-spoken, very much in command of herself. She appeared in good health and good spirits. When drinks were offered, she ordered sherry and sipped it demurely. She gave the impression that she would not interfere in the least with her husband's business obligations. The personnel man was impressed, and partly as a result of the fine appearance she made, the husband got the job.

The personnel man was correct in assuming that the wife would not interfere with the husband's business, nor would she embarrass his employer by getting drunk in public. In truth, she had only one interest in life—painting. As long as she had brushes and a palette in front of her, she did not care whether her husband performed successfully or not. In fact, she did not care about the management of her home, the care of her children or anything else.

On his new job, the husband often appeared at the office late. Finally his superior discovered that the man felt obliged to make his young children's breakfast each morning before getting them off to school, doing the dishes and making the beds. The corporation's personnel man had failed to realize that a woman addicted to painting can be as irresponsible as one addicted to other things, and that one passion carried to extremes is as bad as another.

Ironically, many of the worst examples of modern fatherhood give the impression at first glance of being perfect husbands and fathers. For example, a government official was considered an exemplary father. A poor boy who had worked his way through college and law school, he rose steadily in the legal profession and was finally called to an important administrative position in Washington. All who know him—newspapermen, members of his own political party, even members of the opposition party—agree that here is a competent, dedicated, thoroughly honest public servant whose opinions are worthy of respect. Moreover, he has none of the traditional vices. He drinks most moderately, betrays no interest in any woman other than his wife and would not know how to place a bet on a horse if he wanted to.

However, he has the modern vice that so often poses as virtue; he overworks. He has wrapped himself so thoroughly in his job that it is virtually all he thinks about day and night. He is out almost any evening, at his office, at a business conference or at a social affair connected with his job. On Saturdays he may play golf for recreation, but he invariably plays with professional associates, and somewhere on the golf course business matters will be discussed. Even on Sundays, which most family men spend at home, he is at his office clearing up work he was unable to get to during the week. In fact, he often comments that he prefers working on Sundays because he is not interrupted by phone calls and personnel problems that arise in his department.

His wife and two children seldom see him. He knows almost nothing of their problems and difficulties because they have learned that he is always too busy to concern himself with them. Basic questions—what schools they should attend, how to discipline them, what to do about their religious education, where they should spend their summers—are left to Mother. Father wants nothing to do with them.

He is not wholly blind, and he knows he is not doing for his wife and children what a normal husband and father is expected to do. He sighs, apologizes and says he wishes his job did not make it impossible to spend more time with his family. He is simply lying to himself. The truth is that he chooses to make his job so demanding that he has no time left. He really does not want to be close to his family and to grapple with the problems of his children's upbringing.

This man is running away from his responsibilities as a husband and father. But he has found an escape which seems socially acceptable. He can even picture himself as a martyr and have some people believe that he is compelled by factors beyond his control to neglect his responsibility to his wife and children.

Moonlighters—men who take second jobs at night, on week ends and on holidays to augment the family income—often seem to be conscientious husbands and fathers. Here they are, working like beavers to provide a more attractive home, a better car, better clothing, more efficient household appliances for their family.

What could be more dutiful? But again the truth is that husbands who take second jobs are often motivated less by the unselfish desire to do more for their families and more by the desire to find an excuse to get away from home. Working at night is more agreeable than returning home to keep Johnny and Mary from squabbling, to help Johnny with his homework and to face meetings of the Parent-Teachers Association.

But even men who come home every night can be "runaway husbands." One wife said, "When my husband comes home from work, he grunts a word of greeting to me and the children if he's in a good mood, then places himself on the sofa and hides behind the newspaper until dinnertime. At dinner, about the most stimulating remark he has made during the past year has been, 'Please pass the potatoes.' After dinner, he sits down in front of the television screen. He has his favorite programs for the night all thought out in advance and nobody can say a word while the set is on. So it goes, night after night. He is home in body, all right, but he might as well be in Outer Mongolia as far as his family is concerned."

Since today's young men have much less dedication to the responsibilities of fatherhood than earlier generations had, it seems inevitable that more men actually leave home when faced with responsibilities they do not wish to assume.

A man I will call Joseph B is typical of the fathers who run away physically as well as psychologically. He was the product of overprotective parents who believed nothing was too good for their son. All through his childhood they did everything to make his life easy. When he began school they helped him with his homework every night and often even found themselves doing his arithmetic problems while he watched television out of the corner of his eye.

When his teachers complained about his conduct and scholastic accomplishment, they said the teachers "misunderstood" their child. When he played games, they tried to make sure his playmates did not damage his ego by defeating him.

In brief, they trained him to avoid as much responsibility as he could. And after twenty-two years of indoctrination they turned him loose on an unsuspecting bride. From the beginning of the marriage the girl found herself not only working to augment his meager income but even taking the responsibility for all their financial obligations.

When she became pregnant, her doctor told her that she must quit her job and get plenty of rest if she were to avoid a miscarriage. Suddenly the burden of caring for his family fell upon Joseph's shoulders. It would have been difficult enough for this youth to care for himself alone, much less a wife and child. When he realized he would have to take a part-time job in addition to his regular position to maintain the standard of living he and his wife had become accustomed to, he simply disappeared.

His parents had a ready explanation for his conduct. It was all his wife's fault for getting pregnant and for expecting him to take on the responsibilities of fatherhood. They remained sublimely blind to the fact that they had prepared him throughout his entire childhood and young manhood for just this action. They had shown him how to avoid responsibility at every stage in his development.

Whatever form it takes, a father's absenteeism throws added burden upon a wife. If she accepts the burden, she has no alternative but to become the effective head of the home. When she is forced to move into this vacuum and to assume many of the functions of the male, she cannot help but take on more of the traditional characteristics of maleness. When men complain about women's increasing loss of femininity, therefore, they should realize that this is often a necessary reaction to a father's functional abdication.

6

EMANCIPATION — FOR WHAT?

MORE AND MORE WOMEN ARE GOING BACK TO WORK AFTER THEIR children are born or have left infancy. In 1890 only 5 wives out of every hundred in the United States were employed outside the home. By 1950 the proportion of working wives had quadrupled and there were 20 in a hundred. Today the figure is about 35 in every hundred. As older women who believe "a woman's place is in the home" die off, the percentage of working wives and mothers continues to rise rapidly. More than half of all the women in the labor force are married, and this percentage also has risen steadily over the years. More than half of all working mothers have children under eighteen.

A clear pattern has emerged. The typical young woman works after she is married and holds her job, with her husband's approval, until she is well advanced in pregnancy. It is not unusual for a woman to plan to take her vacation at the time she expects to have her baby. If she has a three- or four-week vacation, she may try to be back at work without losing a day. Or she may take a few extra weeks off after childbirth and then return to the daily grind, while her mother, mother-in-law or other relative begins the life-long job of caring for her baby.

Even if she quits her job to give birth, as the majority of women do, she usually does so with the idea that she will be back on the payroll in a few years. Some mothers remain home only during the first years of the child's life and then arrange for him to attend nursery school as soon as he is eligible so they can go back to work. Most mothers dutifully remain at home until their child completes elementary school.

But when the youngster is in high school, more and more mothers reason, they are no longer needed at home all day. So off to work they go. Looking ahead a few years, ambitious mothers may conclude that it will be impossible to pay for a college education out of family savings or their husbands' current income. If Johnny is to get his highly prized chance at a college education, his mother may think she will have to work to pay for it.

The rise of the working woman is by no means an American phenomenon. It is happening everywhere. Even in Germany, where the tradition that the woman attends exclusively to children, church and kitchen was born, the trend has been noticeable. Partly as a result of the tremendous loss of men's lives in two world wars, the German woman has found a place waiting for her in industry. If she has inherited a family business, she may have found that the only way to keep it going is by managing it herself. According to *The New York Times* (May 25, 1964), of a native German labor force of nearly 22 million, 33 percent are women. While most of these, naturally, are employees, 7.4 percent are actively occupied in the ownership or management of factories or other businesses.

Among the factors which contribute to the movement to full-time outside jobs for mothers is the strange attitude that many moderns have regarding housework and homemaking. Housekeeping is regarded, by white American women, as the lowest of careers. Even the most poorly educated girl seems to think that taking care of someone else's home is beneath her. It violates the fundamental principle of the American dream: one generation must rise above the preceding one, and standing still is the unpardonable crime. Consequently, women will work in factories performing routine, tedious chores hour after hour, day after day, and believe that they are a few rungs higher on the ladder than if they were helping make someone's home a more agreeable and pleasant place for its occupants.

The American domestic is therefore either Negro or a foreign-born white who speaks English badly and cannot get another kind of job. When these whites learn the language and discover the low esteem in which their jobs are held, they move into factories as well.

Since the paid houseworker is almost at the bottom of the social scale, wives and mothers understandably hold the work in low esteem. As one young woman commented, "If I told my husband I wanted a job dusting furniture, scrubbing floors and washing diapers in somebody else's home, he'd think I was crazy. But the furniture there probably is no dustier, the floors no dirtier and the diapers no messier there than they are in my own home. What is it that horrifies my husband if I do this work in somebody else's home, but makes me a heroine if I do it in my own?"

Among working women are many who married without dimly realizing the responsibilities involved in maintaining a home and bringing up children. Such a bride based her ideas of childcare on games she once played with her dolls rather than on the realities. She had visions of clean, cuddly babies who always cooed and never cried; of her husband coming home each evening with a smile and a bouquet of flowers, prepared to spend four or five hours chatting with her. Her home would be the kind shown in a home-and-garden magazine, a spotless love-nest with a white picket fence which stayed neat and trim without effort.

It was a rude awakening to return from the hospital with her infant and discover that caring for a baby is not like caring for a doll. She was soon overwhelmed by all the chores she had never anticipated. She began to think that life was cheating her because marriage, home and family were not the paradise she had dreamed of. In fact, they seemed just the opposite, and she ran to a job to escape from what had become a prison.

Another typical working mother is the woman who has what she considers an unhappy marriage. She wants everything to go her way and discovers it will not. Perhaps having tried without success to remake her husband, she has finally realized that one cannot really change a person. Or she may be unhappy for other reasons. Her husband may be an alcoholic and she cannot stand the constant strain of watching him drink himself into oblivion time after time. Or he may be a compulsive gambler who earns a wage his family could live on comfortably but who cannot wait to run to the race track with his weekly paycheck, leaving them to scrape along as best they can.

The woman with an unhappy marriage or home situation, real or imagined, becomes more and more depressed with the state of things at home. She finds herself constantly thinking about her problems, and they keep intruding when she tries to sleep. The wife in such a plight may have suggested that she take a job, only to have her husband oppose her, not out of any concern for her welfare, but because he thinks his own stature will be lessened if his friends and relatives suspect that he cannot support her. If the problems persist, however, she may take a job whether he likes it or not.

Another kind of working mother is the one who feels inadequate about her education, social demeanor, clothing or poise. This woman thinks she is considered a nobody by her neighbors. She may not have the money or interest to take courses in night school or charm school to improve her knowledge, appearance or personality but she still wants to make something of herself. Perhaps she looks for a job where she can meet other people and impress them more than she has been able to impress those who already know her.

Regardless of what we may say about the home as the ideal place for wives, we must recognize that work is a form of therapy for such people. It is an escape from an unpleasant or unbearable life at home, and it allows them to take their minds off their troubles for at least a few hours a day.

One may wish that such women had within themselves the power to solve their problems, instead of running from them. Yet sometimes the solutions are beyond their reach. A woman has little or no power to change an alcoholic husband who ignores her pleas and those of other relatives, friends, co-workers, perhaps even his clergyman, to stop drinking. By remaining idle, with little else to occupy her mind, she might well endanger her sanity. As one mother replied, when asked whether her two small children should be in a nursery school while she took a secretarial job, "My children are better off this way than if I were put in a mental institution."

But if a mother with young children must work to preserve her sanity, she probably was completely unprepared for marriage and had a woefully inadequate understanding of what is needed to make a marriage work. For example, in most cases the wife of an alcoholic was given ample evidence before marriage that her prospective husband was more attached to drink than is considered normal. The woman who now can't stand to have children screaming all day long probably never took time before marriage to consider what patience a mother needs to bring up a child. The girl who expected to ascend to Cloud Nine at the altar and never again return to earth could have profited from a short course in marriage, which would have revealed the difficulty of uniting two people of different sexes, from different home backgrounds and with different outlooks on life without ever having any conflicts between them.

Since the married mothers in the cases cited above are using work as an escape, perhaps such women really do not want to work and would not do so if conditions were different—if they could get along better with their husbands, if they could manage a more successful and peaceful household, and so on. The fact that such women flee from their homes into offices, stores and factories indicates a failure somewhere in the home, and this in turn suggests a failure in their preparation for marriage. If we wanted to treat this matter of working mothers rationally, therefore, we would not encourage them to work, as many people do, but we would instead try to prevent those conditions that cause mothers to flee from the home.

There is much evidence that the steadily increasing number of mothers holding full-time jobs is not due to their desire to raise the family standard of living. For after a mother pays the taxes on her income, the cost of a baby-sitter or nurse to care for her children when she is away, the expenses of traveling to and from work, dressing suitably, buying lunches and paying for other services such as laundry which would not be necessary if she remained at home, she may actually have very little money left over to raise the standard of living.

More often than working mothers will admit even to themselves, they take outside jobs to establish a personal independence. By proving that she can support herself the working wife improves her bargaining position. It is easier for her to express herself fully and to get her way in family affairs if she knows—and if her husband also knows—that she is not economically dependent upon him.

To some extent, of course, a wife's sense of economic independence is a good thing. The wives of a few generations ago usually had no respectable way of obtaining an independent income. Because they had no economic freedom, they had to put up with their husbands regardless of how they were treated.

The man who would be a tyrant in his home must think twice if he realizes that his wife has the power to go her independent way if necessary. In many cases, the fact that the wife can stand on her own feet contributes to marital harmony. However, a strong-willed woman may use her economic independence as a means of dominating her marriage and as a threat to hold over the head of her husband. Just as we see less and less of the dependent wife, we see more and more of the independent one.

Business management magazines such as *Business Week* have warned that a married woman employee may use a job as a kind of emotional weapon against her husband, and that this is a frequent cause of trouble both in the home and in the office, plant or shop. Many examples can be cited.

One attractive woman in her late twenties works as a secretary to an executive of a metropolitan newspaper. He gives her a great deal of freedom. She can often work at night if she chooses to, and take time off during the day. If she has a disagreement with her spouse, she just rolls over when the alarm rings in the morning and lets him prepare his own breakfast and go off to work. She can also find it necessary to work late at night, thus avoiding returning home to prepare his evening meal. To add fuel to the flames, late on such evenings, she will return home smelling of liquor and reporting on the excellent meal she has eaten at the expense of her employer or one of her fellow employees (male).

Naturally the husband is upset. He suspects her of deliberately seeking affairs with other men, but he cannot prove anything because she claims her activities are necessary for her to keep her job. Since she earns almost as much as he, and since her income enables them to live in an attractive apartment and to enjoy many luxuries, he does not want her to quit her job, and yet he knows that she uses it to achieve a dominant position in their marriage.

There is evidence that the typical wife works less to keep the wolf from the family's door and more to increase luxuries her family enjoys or to obtain satisfactions which she does not find at home. A 1964 study made by the National Industrial Conference Board (*The New York Times,* May 2, 1964) disclosed that in nearly 45 percent of the nation's families with incomes of $10,-000 a year or more, the wife works outside the home. This group represents 20 percent of all families in the country, but they wield about 45 percent of the buying power in the nation. Thus the economic prosperity of the United States is to a large extent derived from the fact that the wife is a wage earner. In itself this factor would seem to assure that the powers in government, whose tenure of office depends in large part on the nation's prosperity, will encourage more women to work.

Another factor that contributes strongly to this trend is that the working wife is much more common in younger families than in old ones. The population still consists of large numbers of men and women who reached maturity with the belief that once a woman becomes a mother, she should not leave her home. As these old-fashioned women die off, the percentage of women who consider it natural to work will increase. In the $10,000-and-up income bracket, some 60 percent of the family heads are between thirty-five and fifty-five years of age. The number of two-income families under thirty-five has increased markedly year by year.

All in all, therefore, we can expect the trend of the working mother to intensify in the future. I do not see any evidence, either in the desire of husbands and wives themselves, or in the economic state of the country and the influences exerted by the most powerful and articulate forces in society, that the employment of wives and mothers will decline.

What will be the effect of all this upon the women involved? For what, exactly, are they being "emancipated"? And what about their children?

While granting freely that many educated women want more intellectual stimulation in their daily lives than is provided by the routine of childcare and housekeeping, one may also wonder whether the typical working mother is truly better off than the one who stays at home.

First, we must face the reality that most women are not profoundly interested in an intellectual life. Nor are they deeply engrossed in cultural matters. One need go no farther than the television ratings to establish this point. When an hour-long program dealing with the inane antics of hillbillies is one of the most popular programs on the air, along with cheap westerns and mass-produced murder mysteries and private-eye programs, we must conclude that most people are not truly interested in intellectual challenges. The cheap and tasteless is almost invariably most popular with the masses.

Let us remember, therefore, that when we talk about the discontented housewife who needs fulfillment in a job, we are talking about a very small minority of women. At this point I must emphasize that there is no indication that the taste of the masses of women is any worse than that of their husbands. In many homes it will be higher; but that is still not saying very much.

For most women, taking a job outside the home may be the beginning of a lifetime of double drudgery. If there is one characteristic of our modern way of life, it is the idea that our living standards cannot stand still but must rise continuously. We must look forward to more luxuries in the future, no matter how well off we may be today. The idea of lowering our standard of living is unthinkable. Even young couples starting out in marriage accept only with the greatest reluctance the idea that their comforts will be fewer than their parents', even though their mothers and fathers may now be enjoying the fruits of a whole lifetime of saving. Young couples think that they too deserve the newest-model cars, fully equipped kitchens and expensive summer vacations. There is no turning back; indeed, they are unwilling to take even one step backward. But this desire to keep moving ahead and never to settle for less than you have known is not confined to young people. It is characteristic of men and women of all ages.

What is the point of all this? Simply that once a family establishes a certain standard of living, it will resist any effort to lower it. In concrete terms this means that once a husband and wife become accustomed to living on an income produced by both persons, there is an almost irresistible desire to continue living on that income level. So the wife who starts working had better recognize that for the rest of her life she will be under pressure to continue producing a second income. She may be superimposing a permanent second job on the job of being wife and mother. Men who go to business every day describe themselves as being in a rat race. In truth, the real rat races are often run by the wives who strive to do two jobs instead of one.

A typical woman in this situation works as the secretary to a large corporation executive. She is a highly competent typist, stenographer, secretary and general assistant—what newspaper classified ads call a "girl Friday." Unfortunately, her general competence, while an asset in business, is her undoing in private.

She is married to an amiable man she met when both were college undergraduates. If he has any ambition in life, it is to do as little work as possible. In college she found herself doing the research for and often even writing his term papers. Through an adroit choice of easy courses and the indulgence of several kind-hearted professors, he finally received his diploma. A friend got him a job as a clerk in a shoe store. He found the work congenial —especially because it gave him the opportunity of playing in the bowling league, joining his fellow clerks in the drinking that usually followed, and engaging in the tension-free life which people who lack ambition often achieve. Meanwhile he married the girl, and naturally she began to work.

They realized they could not live as they wanted on his salary alone. So she kept working as long as she could when she became pregnant. As soon as her baby was born, she turned the infant over to her mother and returned to work. A few years later, despite her best efforts to prevent it, she became pregnant again. She took a leave of absence for six weeks, which was all the time off she could afford, to have the baby and to recuperate.

The children are now seven and ten years old respectively. If they are to be clothed, fed and housed decently and if anything is to be set aside for their college education, the mother knows that she is the one who must do it. Not long ago she sat down wih pencil and paper and discovered that her husband's contribution to the house (after he took out money for bowling, cocktails, office parties and other nights out with the boys) barely covered the cost of his room and board. He is really little more than a paying boarder—and not a well-paying one at that.

Given his irresponsibility to begin with, it is difficult to say precisely how things could have been different. Yet there is a strong possibility that if this woman had not willingly taken on all the responsibility she did, her husband might have been forced to fulfill duties which were rightfully his. As things stand now, however, she is saddled with the obligations of both parents. She is, in effect, both father and mother to her children, and her husband is like an eldest child.

It takes an unusual woman to resist becoming embittered at the realization that her husband has turned all the burdens of family life over to her, while remaining himself as free as a bird. This particular woman has turned into a chronic griper. She belittles her husband at every opportunity, and a day seldom passes when she does not tell him she thinks he is lazy, shiftless and incompetent. What probably infuriates her most of all is that, ironically, mutual friends see him as a smiling, inoffensive individual who is always ready for a good time, while she always seems to be throwing a wet blanket on his efforts to enjoy himself. Many friends think he has the patience of Job to put up with her.

What, then, is a reasonable attitude to take on this question of working wives?

1. I do not think there is anything wrong with a wife's working if she has no small children to require her care. In fact, it could even be recommended that a childless woman take employment—or develop other outside interests—for her own emotional health. As a general rule a couple without children occupy a small apartment which may take no more than an hour a day to maintain. A wife cooped up in a flat all day with nothing constructive to do is a candidate for boredom, if nothing worse. She and her husband would be better off if she found interesting work offering her intellectual challenges and the opportunity to associate with other people.

(It would seem unnecessary to remark that a childless husband whose wife works should also engage in gainful employment. However, such is the state of affairs in our mixed-up world that some young men are content to let their wives go to business, while they spend their mornings sleeping off their excesses of the night before, and their afternoons on the golf course or at the race track. So it must be said that the husband should work as well as his wife.)

2. A mother could work if her children are old enough to get along without her. A mother's presence is essential to a child until he goes to school, at about the age of six or seven. It is highly desirable until he enters high school. In general a mother can care for her child better than any paid substitute, even if she does not keep a spotless home or prepare the most appetizing meals. By her very attention she tells her child that she cares for him. A paid housekeeper no matter how competent is not the child's mother—and the child knows it.

In a few cases a mother of a preschool child might be better off working. If she must work to provide the necessities of life for her family, she really has no alternative. When the father is dead or missing from the home and the family has no other provider, the mother must go to work to keep the home intact.

In a majority of cases, however, mothers who think they must work are selling themselves a bill of goods. At least half the mothers of small children who work outside the home do so not because they really need the second income but because they find the task of taking care of their little ones is boring and disagreeable.

Of course many of these mothers will disagree emphatically if you tell them they really do not need the money. They tell themselves that they need it in order to justify what they are doing, for they well know that their children are being deprived of the care they are entitled to have. Sometimes they can make long lists of things they think they must have—but which they could do without quite easily.

A mother I will call Mrs. P holds a job in a travel agency to supplement her husband's good income as a department head in a large discount store. She has two children aged five and seven and she hires a nurse full time to care for them. Although the cost of paying the nurse amounts to more than half her own salary, Mrs. P insists she must work for economic reasons. She has a long list of needs: Her family must live in a more expensive apartment in a better section of the city than they could afford on her husband's salary alone, even though they could live in modestly comfortable circumstances on his income. The family must have a large, late-model, eight-cylinder car with three hundred horsepower, even though a car costing half as much to buy and operate would get them where they want to go just as quickly. They must have "nice clothes," even though her children's caretaker finds it difficult to choose what they should wear from the abundance of clothing they possess. They must take long vacations at expensive resorts. Mrs. P thinks her neighbors and friends would be shocked if her family chose to "rough it" one summer and lived at inexpensive, out-of-the-way motels and camping grounds.

This wife refuses to acknowledge that these things she lists are really not necessities at all. They are luxuries. Millions of people live comfortably on considerably less than her husband earns. The truth is that she doesn't want to be with her children. They bore her. She sees no challenge in educating them or in serving as the finest influence they can have.

On other grounds, however, it may be questioned whether Mrs. P is wrong in working to escape from her children. For she would be so resentful if she were forced to stay with them that she would probably make their lives a hell. In this case almost any substitute mother is better than the real one. The mistake this woman made was in becoming a mother at all.

Elementary school children (those up to the age of fourteen or so) need the security of knowing that a parent will be there when they come home from school. Often a child will run into a house, toss his books on a table, shout, "Mom, I'm home," and run out again. When he does even this, he is telling his mother it is important to him to feel he has made contact with her.

Some mothers of elementary school children have their cake and eat it as well; they give their children the security of a mother-managed home and work at the same time. A common way of doing this is to take a part-time sales job in a department store, where the busiest hours are those when children are at school and their mothers have time to shop. A typical mother drops her second-grader off at school at nine o'clock, reaches the department store that employs her before it opens at nine-thirty, quits work at three and picks up her child at three-fifteen. The child is just as well off emotionally as one whose mother is at home all day.

3. Regardless of her children's age, the mother who works should not do so in order to compete with her husband as the family provider. Obviously a wife has to be the main breadwinner when, for health or other reasons, the husband cannot give the family the real (not imaginary) necessities of life. Here it is a matter of necessity, and no competition is intended. I am thinking rather of one mother who told a friend that she was "damn tired of having to take the nonsense" she took from her husband and that she was getting a job so she could tell him to "go to hell" whenever she felt like it. She found work at a good hourly wage and then made it her business to work overtime as often as possible. The first time her wages exceeded her husband's, she came home, displayed her earnings to her husband in front of her children and then thumbed her nose at him. "From now on, Mister," she said, "you watch your step or I'll toss you out on your rear."

In another home husband and wife both work and jest about their relationship, but at best their children are growing up with confused attitudes. Both work by the hour, and his wages may be higher one week and hers may be higher the next week. "The boss in this house," they joke, "is the one who made the most money the week before."

4. A mother's decision to work would be justifiable if she can perform a great public service by doing so. With rare exceptions, however, the greatest service a mother can perform is to give her own children the benefit of her presence, care and attention. To paraphrase the Gospel, What does it profit a woman to serve the whole world and yet suffer the loss of her own children?

Many women active in public service are highly respected publicly, yet miserable failures as mothers. This is such a common thing that there is even a well-worn stereotype of the woman who is so busy running the world day and night that her own home drifts dangerously and her own children are lost without a rudder.

Not long ago a nineteen-year-old boy got drunk at a party, stole an automobile so he could take a girl to a secluded park and had an accident on the highway in which both he and the girl were seriously hurt. Police called the boy's home at midnight, but neither the mother nor father was there. The father was out of town on a business trip and the mother was attending a meeting of representatives of social agencies who were trying to work out a program to curb juvenile delinquency in the slums.

When the police finally contacted the mother at two A.M., her first reaction was outrage. How dare they charge that any son of hers could be guilty of such conduct? There had to be some mistake. Maybe somebody was claiming to be her son and had given a false name. Or were the witnesses lying? The driver of the other car involved in the accident— What sort of person was he? What was his family's background? She explored all the possibilities she could think of, and when the police continued to insist that it was her son who had done the deed, she broke into tears. What had gone wrong? To a bystander the answer was easy. She had been so busy trying to run others' affairs that she had no time for her own son.

The young man underwent psychiatric treatment. It soon became obvious that he had no contact or communication with his parents. He believed that there was no one in the world who really cared about his welfare. He lived in a richly appointed home in a lovely community and had every creature comfort, but he lacked what he needed most of all—the intimate, day-by-day communication with parents who took an interest in what he was doing.

It may seem trite to say so, yet it cannot be repeated too often: No one can care for a child like his mother. When she decides to bring a life into the world, she also accepts the responsibility to give her child the constant care he needs to become a happy, well-adjusted adult. The term "responsible parenthood" should relate less to the number of children a mother may bear and more to the protection and direction she gives them.

7

THE PILL'S LONG SHADOW

FOR MOST PEOPLE, DECEMBER, 1954, PROBABLY HAS LITTLE OR NO special meaning. But to future generations it may become known as a milestone in the history of the human race.

At that time two doctors began to administer large doses of a compound closely related to the hormone progesterone to fifty childless women who volunteered for a study to determine whether or not they could be made pregnant. The compounds, called progestins, were given in daily doses of ten to forty milligrams for twenty successive days of each menstrual cycle. A surprising result occurred: During the twenty days that this drug was taken, there was almost a total postponement of ovulation. It was almost certain, therefore, that *as long as these drugs were taken regularly, no pregnancy could occur.* As soon as the drugs were discontinued, the pregnancy rate shot up dramatically.

Here, developed by two doctors working together, Dr. Gregory Pincus of the Worcester Foundation for Experimental Biology and Dr. John Rock of the Reproductive Study Center in Brookline, Massachusetts, was a remarkable treatment with an almost awesome potentiality: a drug that could be used in one way to enable women to engage in intercourse without becoming pregnant, and in another way to improve infertile women's chances of having a child.

In April, 1956, large-scale studies were begun. These progestins in pill form were given to large numbers of women in San Juan, Puerto Rico. Similar field trials were conducted later in Haiti and in several cities in the United States. Several thousand women were given the pills for twenty successive days each cycle, month after month. Many of these women had had babies almost every year. But once they began to take the pills regularly, pregnancy did not occur regardless of how many times they had intercourse.

The contraceptive pill may therefore be regarded as the first really sure contraceptive. Since then, another sure device, even easier to use, has been developed. This is the intra-uterine ring. Made of plastic or other inexpensive material, once it is inserted in the vagina, it can remain in place for years. It effectively blocks the union of male sperm and female ova but, so far as is now known, does not interfere with any other biological process.

All through history intercourse and pregnancy have been inseparable. It was because of this connection that parents erected safeguards around their daughters, that scores of religious and civil laws were enacted, and that many of the age-old traditions and customs were developed to govern the relationship between men and women.

With contraceptives that are virtually 100-percent effective, however, a whole era is opening up in man-woman relationships—an era in which basic responsibilities will be revolutionized. The full extent of this revolution is little realized. Yet there is ample evidence that it is vitally affecting the relationships of husbands and wives and, perhaps to an even greater extent, the relationships of unmarried men and women.

Of course the use of contraceptives is not new. For as long as man has known that copulation leads to pregnancy, he has probably made efforts to prevent coitus from having its natural result. But birth control was usually disreputable. In the earliest societies not only were large families considered gifts from the gods, but also they were economically and sociologically necessary. The need to increase population against the ravages of disease, famine and war made the very idea of contraception intolerable. In fact, a husband who suspected his wife of resorting to such means would generally be justified in asking the rulers of society to impose the death penalty upon her.

Since early times, however, there have been prostitutes interested in preventing pregnancy and birth, which curtailed their earning ability. Their efforts ranged from mere superstitious practices to primitive science. The ancient Egyptians considered the dung of crocodiles or elephants, mixed into a paste and applied to the female organs, an effective means of contraception. Early Hebrew prostitutes, with some semblance of logic, believed that by standing upright and shaking the pelvis violently, they could dislodge the male semen from the vagina. The Greeks rubbed alcohol into the vagina after intercourse on the theory that male seed would thus be destroyed.

Truly effective birth control devices have developed as knowledge of the female body functions has increased. By the beginning of the twentieth century, quasi-scientific devices—suppositories, pessaries, douches—were being employed. Perhaps the most widely used method of all was the removal of the penis from the vagina just before ejaculation.

In the past fifty years or so, literally hundreds of improved methods and devices have been offered for sale. There are diaphragms, vaginal jellies, creams, tablets and suppositories of all kinds, dozens of preparations for douches, and a sheath (condom) for the male. In 1931 there was discovered a natural rhythm in women, which means she can conceive only during a period of about four days a month; by abstaining from intercourse during this fertile period she can avoid pregnancy. This is the so-called rhythm method, which meets the requirement of the Roman Catholic Church that no artificial means of preventing conception be used.

All of these devices and methods were effective, at least to some extent. But none was completely sure. Regardless of the method employed, the persons using it always had some uncertainty. The specter of pregnancy always remained in the background, and a delayed menstruation was always a sign for panic.

The contraceptive pill therefore marks a distinct milestone in the history of contraception. As to its effectiveness and safety, here is an analysis by Dr. Alan S. Guttmacher, chairman of the National Medical Committee of the Planned Parenthood Federation of America, from *The Complete Book of Birth Control:*

The evidence of effectiveness of the oral pill as a contraceptive is based on large field tests which have been conducted for three to five years in Puerto Rico, Haiti, Los Angeles, San Antonio, in New York at the Margaret Sanger Research Bureau, and other locations. In all, several thousand women have taken the pill in these tests. Not one patient who took the pills precisely as prescribed—one a day for 20 days each month—became pregnant. This is a record of effectiveness which no other contraceptive has matched.

Because the steroid pills change the way an important body mechanism works, there was much concern in the early days of testing over possible harmfulness. Accordingly, in each of the field studies, special efforts were made—by tissue analyses and other diagnostic tests—to reveal the presence of any dangerous after-effects. All studies demonstrated that the pills are without danger for the period of time that patients have been under the medication which, in the case of the longest study, is more than five years. No abnormalities have resulted in the thyroid, adrenal, or other glands; no evidence of damage to the liver, blood, kidney, or other parts of the body has been observed. Nor is there any indication that the pill has adverse effects on a woman's ability to have a child; when patients in the tests discontinued taking the pills, ovulation was resumed the next month. Women who did not use other means of contraception became pregnant at a normal rate.

One fear voiced at first was that protracted use of this kind of hormone-like drug might cause cancer of the uterus, ovary, or breast. Careful tests designed to reveal such dangers have shown absolutely no evidence that the pills stimulate cancer. It has even been suggested that the number of women in the Puerto Rican test who developed cervical cancer was lower than in a control group who were not taking the pill. This observation has led the American Cancer Society in 1961 to contribute $58,000 to a long-term study to determine if the pills might be useful in curbing cancer.

Obviously no one can guarantee that continuous use of the oral contraceptives over a period longer than five years of tests will be equally harmless. But there is every reason to think so, based on the mass of evidence accumulated thus far.

We have no reason to doubt Dr. Guttmacher's statement. But whether one doubts it or not is not pertinent to this discussion. What is pertinent is that the vast majority of moderns *believe* that the pill is effective. Millions of men and women who, using any other device, would have hesitated to engage in sexual relations because of fear of pregnancy have no such fears with the contraceptive pill. For the first time in the long history of man humans are free to enjoy intercourse with reasonable confidence that they will not be obliged to pay the price of parenthood.

What consequences can we expect as a result of this safe contraceptive?

An obvious effect of its wide use should be a drop in the birth rate. After all, this is its essential purpose. Such a drop is apparently taking place. The United States Public Health Service has substantiated that the birth rate is declining. For example, for a twelve-month period ending in March, 1964, the estimated total of births was 4,087,000. This is a decline of 49,000 from the total recorded for the previous twelve months.

The report stated:

> Analysis of two factors related to the level of fertility—the marriage rate and the age composition of the female population—shed no light on the declining trend of the birth rate that has persisted for over two years. The marriage rate which had remained stable over a long period of time is now showing signs of increase, but it would take some time for this to affect the birth rate. The age composition of the female population, with increasing numbers of women entering the childbearing ages, is also favorable to a higher level of fertility. But fertility indices continued to show a declining trend. The general fertility rate, females aged 15–44, was 104 as compared with 107.2 for March, 1963.

With the effective contraceptive measures now available, this declining birth rate despite earlier and more numerous marriages is to be expected. The unanswered question is, How far will it go? And what problems will it raise in the future?

It now is fashionable to regard a decline in the birth rate as highly desirable. Over the short term, due to the "population explosion" in Asia and Latin America particularly, it doubtless is. But once the contraceptive pills (or still easier birth control methods which may be developed) become widely used, we may face an entirely different problem.

At present certain amounts of intelligence, sophistication and ease of communication are necessary for the pill to be used effectively. Women must know something about how it works. They must be instructed in its use and warned to take it daily, for if they stop using it, their fertility is likely to be greater than before. Moreover, they—or somebody—must pay the cost of the pill, a month's supply of which could exceed a day's wage in undeveloped countries. For all practical purposes this means that, for the immediate future, its general use will be confined to countries with higher levels of education and industrial development. In the poorly developed countries, where the level of education is lower, communications are poor, and the ability to pay for the pills non-existent, its effect is likely to be insignificant, at least for some time.

Therefore we face the prospect that birth rates in the highly developed countries will decline—perhaps markedly—while in the backward areas of the world rates will continue to grow. Those countries that can least afford population increases will be the least affected, and those that can afford them most will be the ones to use this population-reducing device.

One may wonder what the reaction of the most highly developed part of the earth will be, if its population continues to decrease sharply while the rest of the world swells in population, with the incentives and resources for land expansion which that involves. No nation can accept the prospect of suicide. At some time in the future will it be unpatriotic for a couple to use contraceptives when the effect may be to weaken their country while land-hungry neighbors grow ever more populous?

With the real power to choose whether or not to have children provided by the pill, we can expect dramatic changes in the attitudes of husband and wife when they do decide to beget a child. In earlier societies whenever a husband and wife came together the possibility of pregnancy was on their minds, because they did not know there is a safe period in every woman's cycle. Their attitude was to a large extent fatalistic, because to them conception was not a matter of choice. If coitus resulted in pregnancy, that was how things were, and they had to make the best of it.

This is not to say that in earlier times children in large families were unwanted children. They were often wanted very much because they were an economic asset. If the father was a farmer, he could put his child to work in the fields at an early age. The productivity of even a seven-year-old might easily have paid for his upkeep. (The long summer vacation for schoolchildren was begun because farmers wanted their youngsters around the farm.) Even city dwellers would send their ten- or eleven-year-old child to work after school and on Saturdays during the school year and during his summer vacation. Moreover, his schooling ceased when he was twelve or fourteen, when he was expected to start working full time. Thus if a child was a burden in early childhood, he was well on the way to justifying himself economically before his teens.

Today, of course, this has all changed. Far from being an economic asset, the modern child is usually a liability from birth through adolescence and young adulthood, and in some cases until he completes college or postgraduate work, in his mid-twenties. Unless a couple is strongly oriented toward religion, they do not accept unsought pregnancies with a shrug of their shoulders and the consolation that such is the will of God. They are likely to be more resentful of a child who could have been prevented but wasn't than of a child whose coming is regarded as an act of nature which no one could dispute or avoid.

The Planned Parenthood Federation is doubtless right in saying that effective contraceptives mean that there will be fewer unwanted children and more children who are the result of their parents' deliberate desire. The question then will be, What are a couple's reasons for wanting a child? Do they desire to give a human being the gift of life and of disinterested, unselfish love? Or do they want a child solely as a means to a selfish end—the fulfillment of themselves in fatherhood or motherhood?

Most parents will deny that they want children for their own interests rather than for the child's. They point to the amount of time and attention they devote to their children. But in more cases than is generally realized, parenthood has become a status symbol. A man and woman have a child because of what the child will do for them, not because of what they can do for the child.

There is much evidence that modern parents regard the child as an extension of themselves and, like their car or their home, a symbol of their affluence. Their child is less a person than a thing. For example, he may be driven to attend college when he does not really want to go, because his parents do not want their neighbors to think they cannot afford to send him or that he is not intelligent enough, which thus reflects on them. If he does want a college education, they may insist on an Ivy League college so they can boast about it. When he chooses a career they will fight against his preferring a job without prestige. They want their child to wear a white collar in his work whether he is miserable doing so or not.

The existence of an effective contraceptive is also altering the traditional husband-wife relationship. The pill makes it possible for many women to satisfy their desire for complete personal independence even in marriage. In the past pregnancy was often a time of crisis for such wives.

Several years ago a successful businesswoman, married to an ordinary man who had none of her social and cultural accomplishments, became so wrought up when she discovered she was pregnant that she threatened to kill herself. It developed that she feared that during the advanced stages of pregnancy and while taking care of her infant she would have to depend on her husband for care and support. To "demean" herself by showing herself inferior to and dependent upon the male sex was one of the greatest tragedies she could think of. Now such a woman can be fairly sure this fate will not befall her.

Along with the general loosening of moral standards, the contraceptive pill has had an effect on the moral standards of the unmarried. As one who has been in a position to compare young people's attitudes toward sex over a long period of time, I have not yet overcome the eerie sensation I feel when I observe the complete assurance of today's youngsters in defending their "right" to engage in sexual relations. Of course there has always been premarital sex—much more, in fact, than people of earlier generations were willing to admit or recognize. But those who engaged in it would not have dared to defend what they were doing. There was a standard of moral behavior which virtually every member of society accepted even if he failed to live up to it. Young people who violated the standard felt a sense of failure at being unable to realize their ideals. Of course the constant fear of pregnancy added to their concern.

With old deterrents gone, the young almost take it for granted that there will be sexual intimacy, heavy petting at least, if a boy and girl like each other. A twenty-two-year-old girl, Miss S, is typical of the new breed. She has been dating since the age of sixteen. She has gone out with many different boys, and as casually as she accompanied them to a movie theater, she had affairs with them.

When asked why, she bristled, then shrugged her shoulders. "Why not? They were willing and I was willing. I enjoyed it, and I couldn't think of a good reason why I shouldn't."

"But how about your future husband? Didn't you think you should save yourself for him?"

She threw back her head and laughed. "That question is right out of the Victorian Age," she said. "Do you think the man I marry has spent his time like a monk in a cell, saving himself for me?"

The girl went on to explain her philosophy. She is a hedonist, impure and simple. She believes that if the opportunity of pleasure is offered her today, she would be foolish to resist it, because something may prevent her from enjoying it later.

Her philosophy has its roots in the way she was brought up. From her earliest childhood her mother and father thought nothing too good for her. If she wanted something, the fact that she wanted it was reason enough to give it to her. On the rare occasions when they said "No" to her, she sulked and pouted, and they so feared her disfavor that they relented at once. This girl, like so many modern, overindulged children, had never been trained to curtail her momentary impulses for the sake of some long-range goal. When an opportunity for sexual pleasure arose, she reacted as she had been trained to do. She took it.

This story has a sequel. The girl married, but she soon found that the demand of fidelity imposed by her vows was more than she could stand. A few months after her marriage a detective hired by her husband caught her in a compromising situation with a young professional golfer. She is now divorced and playing the field again.

It would be a good ending to this story to say that she is heartbroken over the turn of events and now realizes the error of her ways. Unfortunately this is not so. She seems more determined than ever to exercise complete sexual freedom with whomever she pleases.

This girl is like an increasing number of persons, young and old, male and female who, because of effective contraception, look upon sex as a source of pleasure entirely apart from the institution of marriage or the begetting of children. To Miss S, intercourse is as far removed from moral law as listening to a concert or eating a well-prepared meal. It is something she can do when she feels like doing it. And now, like the enjoyment of music, she can take this pleasure without worrying one bit about the possibility of pregnancy.

If this new sexual equality and freedom is a temporary phenomenon that will change as the pendulum swings in the opposite direction, there are no signs visible yet to indicate that such a swing has begun. All the available evidence leads to the conclusion that young people increasingly favor more sex freedom rather than less.

A survey of the 1964 senior class at Columbia College in New York showed that 83 percent of the students believed in premarital intercourse. Only 13 percent were against it, and 4 percent were undecided about the matter. While the seniors responded to this question with a variety of answers that ranged from outright approval to acceptance of traditional Judeo-Christian teachings, perhaps the prevailing sentiment was that of the student who favored premarital relations only for two people who have "a feeling for each other and have rationally considered the consequences."

When these advocates of premarital sex speak of limiting it to those who have some affection for each other, they reveal their failure to realize that there is really no other kind of sex, that for any sexual relationship to be more than a mere exercise of physical organs, it must contain elements of affection. The prostitute recognizes this necessity when she pretends to be charmed by her purchaser.

What constitutes affection, however, is a question that brings almost as many answers as there are people. One young woman admitted having affairs with more than half a dozen different boys during the span of a school year. When asked if she had any feelings for the boys, she said that each one had seemed to be a person she liked and with whom she could have a "meaningful relationship." Because some affection was present in each instance, she argued, having intercourse was right. Her attitude prompted one person to ask, How many rights make a wrong?

Every marriage counselor has probably encountered evidence of what has been called the contraceptive mentality. This might be described as a state of mind which reduces all questions about sexual intercourse to a simple formula: If coitus can be indulged in without conception, there is nothing wrong with it.

An unmarried twenty-year-old girl admitted taking contraceptive pills regularly for two years. To her, intercourse posed no greater moral problem than did giving a good-night kiss to a boy friend a generation or so ago. She admitted to having had eight or nine lovers. "They were all nice kids," she confided. "They were good fun to be with, but nobody you'd want to marry."

Asked why she had given herself to all of them, she answered, "Why not? They were nice kids. They wanted it, and it was fun. Nobody was hurt, so why make a big fuss over it?"

A married woman whose husband traveled a great deal on business had a similar attitude. She had had affairs with many men during her husband's absences and said that she saw nothing wrong with it. "Of course I love my husband," she said defensively. "These other men mean almost nothing to me. They're just out to kill time, the same as I am."

Ironically, while widespread use of effective contraceptives may virtually eliminate the fear of pregnancy as a deterrent to intercourse outside of marriage, it may intensify another age-old fear, the contraction of a venereal disease.

Until the pill was developed, the most widely used contraceptive device was the condom. It prevented direct contact between the penis and vagina. In many cases these devices were sold not to avoid conception but to avoid disease. Among those most likely to be infected, the unmarried, it doubtless was the most popular device because it was considered the most effective and because it was the most convenient to use, particularly on the spur of the moment.

The expectations of not so long ago that syphilis could be easily eradicated have not been fulfilled. During World War II, Dr. John Mahoney effected quick cures with penicillin treatment for sailors suffering from syphilis. At once penicillin replaced the old, laborious method of weekly injections of bismuth and arsenic compounds over a period of a year and a half. A simple treatment by a physician in his office could cure the disease.

For several reasons, however, syphilis has not been brought under control. It has become difficult to track down carriers of the disease. Although doctors are supposed to report every case of syphilis they encounter, the American Social Health Association polled physicians anonymously and found that almost nine out of ten cases (88.7%) of infective syphilis are not reported. Furthermore, the widespread assumption that a cure for syphilis had been found led to a decrease in efforts to teach young people about the dangers of the disease and how to recognize symptoms in order to insure early treatment if it is contracted.

As a result the best available national figures show a rise in new cases of syphilis since the midfifties at the rate of more than 10 percent a year. For example, 6,261 cases were reported in 1957 and 22,045 cases in 1963.

The increase among teen-agers has been most shocking. From 1960 to 1964, according to Dr. George Jaman, New York City health commissioner, there was a sevenfold increase in the number of new cases of infective syphilis reported among those from seventeen to twenty years old.

These figures do not reflect a local phenomenon. They are duplicated in the statistics reported from all over the country and, in fact, from all over the world. The fact that the pill and the intra-uterine device, as opposed to the condom, permit the male and female sex organs to come together without any barrier means that in the future it will be easier for one person to transmit the disease to another.

These contraceptives may have an equally revolutionary effect upon the way parents view a daughter's premarital sexual affairs. From time immemorial the virginity of their daughters has been a matter of great concern to almost all people. But the basic question is, Why have parents been concerned?

Is it because they wished to avoid the disgrace that might ensue if a daughter failed to produce a show of blood on the marriage bed? If so, the finding of medical science that the hymen can be broken in perfectly innocent ways and the modern attitude that virginity in itself is of no great consequence tend to make this reason less strong today than ever before.

Is it not more likely that parents objected to a daughter's premarital intercourse mainly out of fear that she might shame them by becoming pregnant out of wedlock? There is ample reason to think this is so. The old stereotype of the father throwing his daughter out of his house confirms this. He does not force her into the cold because she has known a man but because she has become pregnant. In other words, he objects not because she sinned but because the world will know it.

If this is true, we might expect parents to adopt a much more indulgent attitude toward premarital sex in the future. Already doctors are finding mothers bringing teen-age daughters for contraceptives on the theory that the child "is going to do it anyway and might as well be completely safe."

Not long ago students at a midwestern state university created such an uproar at an all-night, no-holds-barred party at a motel that police were called to quell the disturbance. They found several couples in compromising positions and took them to jail. The policeman on duty called the father of one of the girls and told him that he had better come bail out his daughter. The father arrived in an agitated state and asked the policeman to describe what had happened. The officer explained that the daughter and a boy friend had been found drunk in bed, playing the radio as loud as it would go. On hearing what had happened, the father sighed audibly. "Thank God," he said. "I thought it was something more serious."

That parents' concern about their daughters' virtue was in the past primarily related to fears of pregnancy is also suggested by the fact that a double standard has existed for thousands of years. Not only has premarital intercourse by sons been condoned; in many circles it has even been encouraged. Some people considered it a father's duty to introduce his son to a house of prostitution.

Even today parents who strive in the most conscientious way to protect the virtue of daughters show a corresponding indifference to the premarital activities of sons. In Latin countries generally, a daughter is closely watched from the time she reaches puberty until her wedding day, but a son has almost unlimited freedom, if not license. It may be an oversimplification to say that the whole reason for this double standard is that daughters can become pregnant while sons cannot, but it is doubtless the major one.

The existence of an effective contraceptive device may have a good effect in helping to decrease the frigidity which affects up to half of all married women. I have in mind cases like that of the twenty-year-old girl, Miss M, whose mother complained that she was unwilling to date men. Although Miss M had a strong desire to marry and raise a family, she found herself backing away whenever a male came too close.

During an interview with the psychiatrist she became violently disturbed, and she shouted at her mother, "When I was fourteen you warned me to keep away from men because they would make me pregnant for their own selfish pleasures. I obeyed you sincerely. Now, after all these years, I cannot change."

Fear of pregnancy often keeps married women from participating in sexual relationship with their husbands as wholeheartedly as they might. There are many known cases of wives who were cold, unresponsive, even utterly unreceptive to their husbands' advances during most of their marriage. When they reached the menopause and could no longer become pregnant, they went to the other extreme, becoming so aggressive and sexually demanding that their husbands could hardly provide the activity they craved.

8

THE
NEXT
STEP:
HOMOSEXUALITY

I HAVE STATED THAT THERE HAS BEEN A MARKED DECLINE IN THE
masculinity of the modern male and in the femininity of the female.
I have said that increasing numbers of boys do not know what it is
to act like husbands and fathers because they have no close example
to guide them. I have said that due to the absence of fathers more
and more girls do not know what it is like to have a loving relationship with a male. Furthermore, I have said that there is an increasing preoccupation with sexual pleasure, a growing idea that everyone is entitled to as many orgasms as he wants, and a now solidly

entrenched notion that sexual enjoyment need have nothing whatever to do with pregnancy and childbirth.

If all these statements are true, one inevitable result should be a great surge of homosexuality—of participation in sexual exercises for their own sake without any relationship whatsoever with procreation. And this surge of homosexuality is exactly what seems to be occurring today.

It is impossible, of course, to state precisely whether there are more homosexuals in modern society than in the past. The difficulty in arriving at precise statistics is illustrated by the fact that the number of homosexual males in New York City has been variously estimated at from 100,000 to 600,000. In *The Sixth Man* Jess Stearn states that one male in six is homosexual—a total of 16,000,000 in the nation. The number of overt homosexuals in the United States—those who have committed homosexual acts at one time or another—is estimated by police authorities at 400,000.

Despite the impossibility of getting exact figures, virtually all well-qualified observers have noted a definite increase in the number of homosexuals in our society. For example, in 1964 the Committee on Public Health of the New York Academy of Medicine issued the first comprehensive study of this subject by a recognized organization representing all branches of medicine. It frankly stated its impression that "at the present time the practice of homosexuality is increasing among the population at large." It added:

Certainly, if there is not more homosexuality than in the past, it appears to be more open and obtrusive. More plays and books are having homosexual characters, and more homosexuals have taken to writing autobiographies. Furthermore, the homosexual seems to have become more formally organized with a central office and a magazine of his own.

These developments stand out in stark contrast with the situation which existed in New York thirty years ago when the subject was less frequently and less openly presented and its votaries rallied once a year to hold their well known Fairies' Ball.

One need only stroll about New York City to observe examples of overt homosexuality that would have been unthinkable twenty years ago. For example, along Third Avenue in the Sixties and Seventies, pairs of men or women stroll along without making any effort to mask their relationship. Numerous well-frequented bars cater exclusively to deviates. Some summer resort areas, such as sections of Fire Island, on the south shore of Long Island, are notorious gathering places for the vacationing homosexual.

Stearn declares that homosexuality is almost commonplace in the United States. He quotes homosexuals as saying that "there is hardly a community of any consequence which doesn't have a park or bus stations where strangers can soon become friends. In some cities the busiest street corners and the smartest hotels are contact centers." Nor are homosexuals only to be found in the largest cities, as is popularly believed. Stearn says that there are many homosexuals in the smallest communities, and it is the usual practice for a deviate in a strange town to head for the local bus station, where contact with others of his condition can be made.

"Often a community is the last to suspect that it may be a harbor for homosexuals," he says. "Long before a stunned citizenry of Waukesha, Wisconsin, was aware of what was going on regularly in one of its most beautiful parks, the homosexual underground was fully alert to the situation. After the arrests of ten men in a series of raids on the park which was also frequented by families on innocent outings, flabbergasted Waukesha police learned that in public washrooms as far away as Milwaukee and Detroit, was scrawled this advice for the knowledgeable: 'Try Frame Park, Waukesha.' "

The homosexual movement has done much to remove the sense of shame that the deviate once felt. Now deviation is flaunted openly. And as the Committee on Public Health reports, homosexuality is even openly advocated as a noble, preferable way of life. Organized homosexuals also claim that their practice is the perfect answer to the problem of the population explosion.

An argument heard frequently today is that each individual has a right to sexual expression and is entitled to use any method which he personally finds satisfying or gratifying. Homosexuals argue that the development of contraceptives has revolutionized the relationship between bisexual intercourse and parenthood so that sex is now for recreation, not procreation. They are joined in this argument by many heterosexual moderns who stress that the sexual act between man and woman is primarily an expression of mutual love and not a means to perpetuate the race.

It is doubtful that there has ever been a time when lesbianism— or what one feminist calls "sex without serfdom"—was as easy to practice as it is today. Until about fifty years ago unmarried women the world over were required to lead sheltered lives. Maiden ladies lived with their parents and then generally found a place to live with a married relative. Nineteenth-century America had a plethora of Aunt Sarahs—elderly women passed over in the marriage sweepstakes who were given a permanent home with the family of a married brother or sister. For the unmarried woman of that time to set up her own home was unthinkable. For one thing, she rarely had a means to support herself; job openings for women in business or industry were difficult to find.

The modern single woman, whether unmarried, divorced or widowed, is usually able to take care of herself. She has no difficulty getting an apartment because, by and large, renting agents have found women to be more conscientious than bachelors about paying the rent monthly and keeping the apartment in good condition. She has no difficulty finding another woman to share her apartment with her. Newspaper classified sections often list dozens of such opportunities.

In this matter at least, women cannot complain that their rights are not equal to those of men who practice a similar perversity. In many places—for instance, in England and in many American states—male homosexuality is punishable by a prison sentence but female homosexuality is permitted without penalty. A common male attitude toward lesbians is rather revealing. A man who condemns the male homosexual without mercy and looks upon his acts with unspeakable scorn often regards female homosexuals with mild amusement.

Society tends to regard female homosexuality as less unnatural than the male variety. For instance, one would not think twice if he saw two women embrace in public. They do it everywhere. Nor is it considered unusual to see women dancing together on dance floors, walking hand in hand on the street, or kissing each other when greeting and taking leave of each other. Men who make similar public displays of affection are strongly suspect.

Moreover, two women may live together for years without ever being suspected of having sexual relations with each other. Sometimes the busy, successful woman who lives with her "assistant" or "secretary" is engaged in a permanent homosexual affair with her, but the relationship is not suspected even by those very close to them. On the other hand, if two men were to set up permanent quarters and to restrict themselves almost exclusively to each other's company, rumors of homosexuality would almost surely begin to fly.

The increase in the number of lesbians actually is quite understandable. The very nature of sexual intercourse involves some degree of male domination. He must want to copulate in order for the act to be completed. She can be passive, indifferent or even opposed to it; yet the act can be accomplished. It is obvious that the woman who refuses to be dominated in other spheres of activity will not find it easy to be compliant in the bedroom.

As Simone de Beauvoir puts it in *The Second Sex,*

Even when she has a good figure and a pretty face, a woman who is absorbed in ambitious projects of her own (or one who simply wants liberty in general) will decline to abdicate in favor of another human being; she perceives herself in her activities, not merely in her immanent person; the masculine desire that reduces her to the confines of her body shocks her as much as it shocks the young boy; she feels the same disgust for submissive females as does the virile man for the passive pederast. She adopts a masculine attitude in part to repudiate any appearance of complicity with such women; she assumes masculine attire, manner, language. She forms with a feminine woman companion a couple in which she represents the male person; play-acting that is, indeed, a masculine protest. But it is a secondary phenomenon; what is primary is the shamed repugnance of the conquering and sovereign subject at the thought of being transformed into fleshy prey. Many athletic women are homosexual; they do not regard as passive flesh a body that denotes muscle, activity, reactiveness, dash; it does not magically inspire caresses, it is a means for dealing with the world, not a mere objective thing in the world; the gulf existing between the body-for-sale and the body-for-others seems in this case to be impassable. Analogous resistance is to be found in women of executive and intellectual types, for whom submission, even of the body, is impossible.

While willful and domineering women are perfectly heterosexual and will cheerfully engage in sex, it is usually on a basis in which they dominate. For example, Catherine the Great sought men lovers but there was never any doubt that she was in control.

Miss de Beauvoir goes on:

This reconciliation between the active personality and the sexual role is, in spite of any favorable circumstances, much more difficult for woman than for man; and there will be many women who will avoid the attempt, rather than wear themselves out in making the effort involved. Among women artists and writers there are many lesbians. The point is not that their sexual peculiarity is the source of the creative energy or that it indicates the existence of this superior type of energy; it is rather that, being absorbed in serious work, they do not propose to waste time in playing a feminine role or in struggling with men. Not admitting male superiority, they do not wish to make a pretense of recognizing it or to weary themselves in contesting it. They are looking for relaxation, appeasement, and diversion in sexual pleasure: they do better to avoid a partner who appears in the guise of an adversary; and in this way they rid themselves of the fetters implied to femininity.

Very often, of course, it is the nature of her heterosexual experiences that leads the active virile woman to make the choice between assuming and repudiating her normal sexuality. Masculine disdain confirms the homely woman in her feeling that she is unattractive; a woman of pride will be wounded by a lover's arrogance. Here we encounter again all the reasons for frigidity already noted; resentment, spite, fear of pregnancy, the trauma of a previous abortion, and so on. The more mistrustful woman is in her approach to man, the more weighty these reasons become.

Lesbianism can never be a completely satisfying way of life, however. The self-contained woman, committed to a struggle with man in which she is determined not to allow herself to be dominated, cannot entirely escape the basic urges of her sex. Even in the most ambitious and briskly masculine of women there lingers a desire for motherhood. The effort to reconcile this desire with the unwillingness to submit to the male sometimes produces some unusual cases.

One woman, successful at managing a business with a dozen men in her employ, could not bring herself to a relationship with a male upon whom she would have to depend for sexual satisfaction. Yet she felt that for her own self-fulfillment she should have a child. She planned her campaign like a general. She took a year's absence from her business, went to Europe, sought out a handsome Latin whom she paid to make love to her, had her baby and returned home with the infant. The future of this boy, who will grow up without a father's influence, in a completely woman-dominated environment, will almost surely involve personal tragedy. Few twisted lives can be forecast so clearly.

Another bizarre example of the desire of the lesbian to be free of men and yet to be a mother is given by two women who lived together harmoniously. The more passive of the two wanted a baby. One day a young, good-looking, happy-go-lucky plumber came to their apartment to repair a leak. This was the beginning of a strange triangle. Although he was a married man, he lived with the two women, and every week he received a cash gift which exceeded the amount he could have earned as a plumber. He slept with the more feminine member of the pair, while the other indulgently encouraged this arrangement. Fortunately, the woman failed to become pregnant, and after six months the lesbians terminated the plumber's employment and sent him back to his wife and his regular trade.

Increasing numbers of homosexuals both male and female have assumed positions of power in the most important area of modern life, the area which influences the attitudes of the rest of the population. They are increasingly active in such fields as communications and can be found in growing numbers on the staffs of newspapers, magazines and press associations. In *The Sixth Man* Jess Stearn writes this about their activities in the world of fashion:

> The average woman little realizes that current smart fashions are often the product of homosexuals who have no appreciation of well-rounded curves.
>
> Under the mass pressure of the homosexual clique dominating the style world, the face of beauty is changing, too. No longer is it fashionable to be rosy-cheeked and laughing-eyed, with a healthy tan and shining round face. Dramatic

planes, with high cheekbones and hollow, haggard cheeks, are the coveted ideal, and circles under the eyes add to the sweet mystery of it all.

Legs with calfs have gone out of vogue, and though busts are fighting their way back to popularity through the valiant effort of the movie queens, they still have no high place in the fashion field.

It is all, observers insist, part of a homosexual design— male and female—to demean and degrade the traditionally American concept of soft, lovely, feminine beauty.

The plot to defeminize the female face and form usually begins with the homosexual designers, who fit their clothes for gaunt, emaciated women. It extends to homosexual or lesbian magazine editors, who hire boyish-looking girls to show these clothes, and is supported by fashion photographers, homosexual or otherwise, who use these models out of preference or to stay in tune. . . . "A girl with a bust just doesn't have a chance in high-fashion modeling," a leading photographer's representative pointed out, "because even if there is a straight photographer or editor who will give her a chance, she doesn't fit the clothes originally styled to a gaunt form."

Stearn declares that the homosexual, with his flare for clothes, has also contributed to shaping masculine fashions. Preferring tight trousers, he introduced narrow-cut blue jeans to appeal to teen-age toughs and slim Ivy League trousers for the more refined. He is responsible for the popularity of leather jackets, broad leather belts, and identification bracelets. These and other homosexual innovations have unwittingly been adopted by rugged heterosexuals.

Homosexuals are also active in the entertainment world—

motion pictures, radio, television and theatre. Stearn alleges that the casting of an unsuspected homosexual as a hero in dramatic presentations may have a greater impact than anyone can imagine. Stearn points out that in the last generation screen stars were the ideal males for many young females, and now the ideal is often a homosexual. "To many in the entertainment business," he says, "it seems a cruel mockery that the love image of some sighing teen-ager should be formed by some beautiful young man who wants nothing more himself than another beautiful young man." As Stearn declares, the social effects of this mass burlesque can be devastating. Where girls once idealized he-men like Gable and Cooper, their daughters now consider some pretty-boy star with wavy hair as their dream man. They may search for this type off screen and discover that what they think is masculinity is really homosexuality.

There also are many homosexual playwrights who generally paint women in a very unfavorable light. There is no sweetness of romance about their female characters, who usually are vicious, conniving mothers and wives. The homosexual playwright is saying, in effect, that a man is a fool to make love to them.

9

THE
LOST
GENERATION

AN ADULT IS THE PRODUCT OF MANY THINGS: THE HORMONES AND organs he was born with, his nervous system, his predisposition to certain ailments, the environment in which he was born and received all his childhood impressions. One of the most important factors is the training and example given him by his parents. To a large extent, therefore, the kind of adult a child will become depends on the influences his mother and father exert on him.

The parent who wants a son to achieve a complete sense of identification of himself as a male, and who wants a daughter to become a full woman in the long-accepted meaning of that term, has it in his or her power to achieve this objective. To do so, however, the parent must resist some strong tendencies in modern life.

When I see a man who is masculine in the real sense of the word—one who accepts the responsibilities of a husband and father, who thinks it his duty to protect and provide for his wife and children—I am reasonably sure that in his childhood he lived closely with and observed intimately a masculine model. Take a woman who dominates her husband and considers herself the real ruler of her home, the one whose decisions about the major questions of family life should be followed, and it is more than likely that she is copying a childhood model, a female who acted in that same way.

That is why I deplore the modern decline of the father's influence. A child needs a mother and father, and if he must grow up without one, he has been deprived. Stated in simple terms, a girl needs a mother to show her how to act like a woman and to offer guidance from her own experience in the girl's problems of growing up. A girl needs a father if she is to have some early understanding of what it is like to love and be loved by a man, and some insight into the specific and distinctive characteristics of the male. Without this experience, she will reach young womanhood not really knowing what a husband expects of his wife or what she has a right to expect of a husband.

In like fashion, a boy needs a father to serve as an example of manhood. The boy needs to see how a man conducts himself in the everyday aspects of living, how he gets along with other men, how he responds to the demands of his job, how he fulfills his responsibility as the chief provider of his family, how he treats his wife and children. The boy needs a mother because it is essential to his

education as a whole person to know the love of a woman, to understand her nature and to learn what pleases and displeases her.
Just as a fatherless girl usually enters marriage in a vacuum, so too
the motherless boy often fails to understand what a true, lasting
and loving relationship with a woman involves.

When the father is absent from the home for long periods, either
physically or psychologically, the situation is charged with potential danger. In such circumstances a mother almost naturally tends
to become too affectionate and protective. Being a woman, she
impresses her own feminine qualities upon her son and favors his
behavior when it appeals to her feminine character more than
to his own masculine one. She may think it not only desirable for
herself but also praiseworthy in him if he showers affection on her.
She may encourage him to talk to her as she talks to other women,
so that his idea of conversation will be taken from the feminine
example.

These dangers are increased in homes where the parents have
been divorced and the mother takes care of the children alone. Unless she exercises firm control over herself she will have a strong
tendency to portray the child's father as the offending partner.
Sometimes even without realizing it she may work to break down
the boy's respect for his father by teaching him in a subtle way that
masculine values are less acceptable than feminine ones.

It is generally in the teen years that one-sided parental love cre-
ates a crisis. The adolescent goes through a stage in which he
strives to establish his identity. Which way should a boy move? In
the direction that his desire for independence and masculinity
leads him? But if he does assert himself in this way, will he be be-
traying his mother, rejecting her, repeating the evil his father did?

[152]

How these questions are answered will to a large extent determine what life the boy will live, and whether he will achieve his potential as a man. If his mother has built up too close a relationship with him and has come to treat him as a substitute lover, he may find it impossible to break away from her. And if he cannot find his maleness as an adolescent, the chances are poor that he will ever do so. He will have been permanently cast in the mold of a Mama's boy.

One of the most conspicuous examples of a person made a homosexual by parents was the seventeenth-century queen of Sweden, Christine. Her father, Gustave Adolphus, had wanted a son, and when his wife gave birth to a daughter, he treated the girl exactly as he would have treated a boy. She became more adept than most males at many sports, but in affairs of the heart she was unable to respond with womanly submission. She was raised deliberately as a male and when the time came for sex, she acted as a male, as the dominant partner, with other females.

The influence of environmental factors in the making of a homosexual is also illustrated by the case of Mr. C. He was the youngest of five children; the other four were girls. With their mother, they held up the virtues of women as ideals for him to follow. He was an overprotected child who was never allowed to act like a real boy. He played mostly with girls during his childhood, and when he did play with boys, his mother remained nearby to warn him against running too fast, lest he fall and hurt himself, and against exerting himself too much, lest he become overtired. He was not permitted to go swimming in a lake like other boys his age, and his mother refused to let him have a baseball bat and glove because she had heard of a boy who had lost his front teeth from being hit in the mouth in a baseball game. The boy was tall and heavy, and when he went to high school, the football coach told him that he had a good chance of making the first team. But his mother had to sign a release for him to play. She refused to do it.

Taught to act and think like a girl, he naturally began to associate with boys in his class who thought and acted as he did. While most of his classmates were at football games, either playing or cheering for their team, he and his companions spent their time sitting around and gossiping, just like his older sisters. Not surprisingly, he drifted into homosexual relationships.

After three or four affairs, Mr. C began to grow despondent. He realized that he was not acting in a masculine way, but the major influences only reinforced his homosexual tendencies. He went to a psychiatrist for treatment.

However, once a person has established a sexual habit and is accustomed to finding physical satisfaction in it, it is very difficult to change. Such may be the case with Mr. C. He is now twenty-two years old. Heterosexual intercourse is an unknown and strange experience for him, and whether he will be able to have normal relationships with a female remains to be seen. His one effort so far was a failure. He was solicited by a prostitute on a street corner, went with her to her room and watched her disrobe, but even with her help, he was unable to arouse any desire for her. Another example of the difficulties of establishing heterosexual relationships once a homosexual pattern has developed is the case of Mr. B. He was introduced to homosexuality at the age of fourteen, when an older boy took him to a park at night and began to play with him. Since that time he has had relations off and on with many different men.

Then he met an attractive girl who he thought would make a

fine wife. She was a somewhat sexy-looking blonde who had been accustomed to having men make passes at her. When Mr. B treated her "like a perfect lady," she began to like him. Nevertheless, during their engagement she grew concerned because he never tried to pet her and appeared satisfied with a perfunctory goodnight kiss. She asked her minister if this was normal. He assured her that she had met an outstanding young gentleman, and that once they were married he would reveal his true masculine colors. "You won't be able to keep him away from you," the minister told her.

On their honeymoon, however, Mr. B found it impossible to achieve an erection with her. They went two years without consummating the marriage. The untouched bride, convinced by now that something was wrong, returned to the minister, and he agreed that it was indeed strange that a husband did not want his wife in all that time. She sought a divorce, despite her husband's desperate pleas and even threats to shoot himself if she left him. She married a man she had rejected years before because he had seemed too ardent. Mr. B now lives with another man.

Because a woman can play a passive role in heterosexual intercourse, it is easier for a practicing lesbian to marry and have a seemingly normal sexual life with her husband. Even so, once a woman has become habituated to achieving sexual relief in one way, it is not easy to give up. Mrs. M is a case in point. Her homosexual relations started in grade school, where she had experiences with classmates and once with a teacher, and continued in high school and college. Although she was very boyish-looking, with an angular figure and her hair cut short and straight in manly style, a young man proposed to her and they were married. She never had any real desire for intercourse with him, yet she managed to keep him satisfied and unsuspecting, partly because he himself did not have a strong sex drive and was content with having intercourse only a few times a month.

She made friends with a woman in her apartment house and began seeing her every day. This woman lived on an inheritance, so the two woman could spend considerable time in each other's company. The husband did not realize what was going on. He considered it strange that she never complained—and in fact generally encouraged him—when he spent an evening at work or out with business associates. One day, however, he returned home in mid-afternoon and found his wife in bed making love to the other woman. They were quietly divorced on the grounds of "cruelty," and the wife moved in with her neighbor.

One of the greatest services that could be done for present and future generations would be the elimination of the consuming fire known as smother love. Smother love is the product of the assumption that children can do nothing for themselves and always need an adult nearby to supervise them, keep them out of mischief and make sure they don't hurt themselves.

In the suburbs smother love sometimes reaches absurd proportions. Even a teen-ager cannot walk to the bus station by himself; he must be driven there by his doting mother. The lad who tries to establish a beachhead of independence by delivering newspapers after school finds Mom all too eager to take him on his rounds by car at the first sign of a sprinkle. If the skies darken, she is waiting outside school with rubbers and umbrella to escort him to the car and drive him home. She stands on the sidelines whenever he plays football to make sure he wears his helmet and his tooth-guard. If, with a strange show of spirit, he gets into a fight with a classmate and comes home with clothes torn or nose bloody, she will storm to the school and demand that the principal put an end to such conduct and, preferably, that he forthwith expel the delinquent who set upon her child.

The typical smother does not think she is doing anything wrong. On the contrary! In her own mind she is the most conscientious of parents. Her only concern is the welfare of her child. She does not realize that by hovering over him constantly, making all his decisions for him and denying him the right to experience the normal give-and-take of human relationships, she is stunting his growth. She is destroying what he needs most of all if he is to lead a normal, satisfying adult existence: the security that comes from knowing he can stand on his own feet and meet the world by himself, without help from Mom or Dad.

Parents' treatment of their child's sexual development greatly affects the ideas of masculinity or femininity he will have when he grows up. Their factual, reasonable and moderate attitudes toward sex are the best assurance that the child will have reasonable, moderate—and acceptable—attitudes of his own when he reaches maturity.

Sex education begins in infancy. The child discovers his sex organs as he explores his body, and his genitals are something to touch and explore, just like his eyes, ears, nose and mouth. Many parents complacently watch a child feeling his nose or putting his fingers into his mouth because they recognize that he is learning about the organs of his body. But let him move his hands to his genitals in similarly innocent exploration, and they become disturbed. Some even slap the child—a response which is certain to focus his mind on that organ and to implant the idea, even at this early stage of life, that there is something inherently dirty and forbidden about it.

Toilet training is a crucial point in a child's sexual development. He associates sex with bodily elimination because the same organ is involved in both processes. If he is made to develop an obsession about toilet training and about always being clean, to avoid the disapproval of those whose affection he wants, he will develop excessively rigid attitudes toward the sex act itself. Many cases of sexual abnormality, frigidity and impotence can be traced to overly severe bladder and bowel training.

Probably every child engages in sexual experimentation after infancy. The three- to six-year-old may feel his genital organs and enjoy the sensation he produces. I find that even the most modern mothers must be told that only if masturbation becomes prolonged and persistent at this age is it abnormal. Then it may indicate that the child is troubled; perhaps he is lonely and insecure, or he may feel a need for love he is not receiving.

Other forms of sex exploration also are frequent in childhood. It is common for little boys and girls to show their organs to one another. In their minds this is no worse than showing articles of clothing, toys or other objects. Some may even attempt some form of contact between organs; this experimentation also is caused by curiosity alone.

During the latency of childhood—from about age six to age twelve or thirteen—children normally associate with others of their sex. Some authors call this time of life the natural homosexual period. An attraction for a member of one's own sex at this age is a common psychosexual development. Freud believed that such a "homosexual" episode might be a step on the path to normal sexual maturity. Usually an attachment of this kind fades away if it is treated calmly and if the child is not ridiculed because of it. Not unless such behavior persists after puberty does it suggest a serious problem, and even then its persistence by itself should not be regarded as a symptom of abnormality. Teen-agers will frequently prefer the company of their own sex. While boys will not express a loathing of females at this age as they might have done a few years earlier, they still will not make much of an effort to be in their company. This is less true of girls, who develop emotionally and physically at an earlier age.

By overreacting to a child's expression of interest in sex, parents may predispose him to homosexuality. One woman who engaged in homosexual practices told me this tale of her early childhood.

When she was seven years old, she and the boy next door went to the basement of her home. She undressed and showed him her body and he did likewise. Her mother caught them in the nude and beat her with a strap, causing black-and-blue marks that lasted for months and a few scars that remain to this day. Then her mother locked her in a dark closet all night. The next morning, her mother told her that if she ever let another boy touch her, she would receive an even worse beating.

The girl grew up with a deathly fear of men. She found it difficult to dance with boys because they would come too close to her. Although she was physically attractive, with such an attitude a normal heterosexual relationship was of course out of the question for her. Lacking another outlet for her sex urges and without religious convictions about the impropriety of using sex outside of marriage, the woman drifted into a homosexual arrangement with an older woman she met in her office. She became a confirmed lesbian, and over a period of fifteen years has had almost a dozen different partners.

Probably more cases of female homosexuality than most people realize stem from badly managed sex education. When a woman finds it difficult to respond to her husband, or to any man for that matter, it is because she thinks intercourse is evil or abnormal or because she has been taught to fear pregnancy or other consequences of the act. For example, the woman who has been led to believe that all men are beasts, who seek only their own gratification, may be especially susceptible to the temptation to engage in sexual activities in which men play no part.

Of course it is a mistake to try to force boys and girls to date before they are emotionally ready. By associating with members of their own sex in their preteens and early teens, they come to know exactly what maleness or femaleness means. They learn to react to situations as other members of their sex react. They develop the same ideals and ambitions as their associates. In brief, they learn to act as persons who will be accepted as men or women in adulthood. The boy who learns to get along well with other boys has an increased sense of his own masculinity. He feels a male among males and considers himself capable of performing various functions expected of men. Likewise the girl who identifies her own aims and ambitions with those of other girls usually has little difficulty in visualizing herself as a wife and mother.

While it is wrong to push children into early dating, it is also wrong to discourage dating when classmates and contemporaries are doing it. In our society this would be around the junior year of high school—age seventeen or so. I will discuss this point at greater length below.

When I say that boys and girls should learn to differentiate between "man's work" and "woman's work," I do not mean that there is an absolutely rigid and unyielding line. A boy should know that washing dishes, preparing meals and cleaning up after them is a chore for females generally, but he should also be prepared to do those jobs if necessary.

A sixteen-year-old boy, the oldest of three sons, came home one day to find his mother ill in bed with a high fever. His younger brothers, of preschool age, had had no lunch, and the mother asked the sixteen-year-old to make sandwiches for them. "But I don't know how," he said. "You've always made them for me." This lad was not displaying masculinity but merely incompetence.

It will not harm a boy's development—on the contrary, it will help it—if he at least learns how to cook a hamburger, wash dishes, run a washing machine and press a shirt. The knowledge that he can do these things will increase his self-reliance and his self-confidence. Nor will it turn a girl into a masculine figure if she can hit a tack into a wall and hang a picture in her room.

But such chores should not be habitual. As a general rule it harms a son's masculinity if he must always don an apron and wash or wipe the dishes after a meal, just as a girl's sense of femininity is diminished if she must scrub down the walls of a room when there is a boy in the house who could do the job.

An extreme case of misidentification involved a boy and girl brought up in a home where every chore was considered to apply to both of them. One week the son washed the dishes while his sister dried them; next week she washed and he dried. He was assigned the task of dusting the furniture one week, while she scrubbed the kitchen floor; next week he scrubbed while she dusted. In high school they received identical allowances and were still expected to contribute identical services to the home.

When the boy began dating, he did not see why he should pay for his girl friend's entertainment. Consequently all his dates were on a Dutch-treat basis, with him paying for his share and his girl friend paying for hers.

When he married he acted just as his training had prepared him to act. He expected his wife to work and he expected to help out around the house. After their first child was born, his wife returned to work. Now the baby is cared for equally by both parents. As far as the infant is concerned, there is no difference between the male parent and the female parent. In such a home it will be a major miracle if he develops any understanding of what it means to be a male. Such an environment is a climate for the making of a homosexual.

The girl in this family has also married—three times already. The first two husbands were determined to assert their masculinity to some extent, were unwilling to do the housekeeping chores she demanded of them and expected her to act like the traditional wife and homemaker. They finally divorced her. Her third husband is someone like her brother. Soon after the wedding she became seriously ill for several months and required hospitalization. When her own savings had been used up for the medical bills, her husband refused to dig into his own nest egg for her additional expenses. They had lived together on a share-and-share alike basis, and this situation, which called on him to give more than his share, was something he had not bargained for. He took a job in a different state and left his bedded wife to her own devices.

In considering the factors which tend to neutralize the sexes, the modern school system shares some responsibility. In times past—and still, to a large extent, in Europe—boys' teachers were almost always men. They instilled male standards in their pupils. The boy who was thought a sissy—the one who always sat quietly, never joined in horseplay, was always neat and clean, prim and proper—was likely to be the least popular boy in his class not only with classmates but with his teacher as well. Transferred to a class with a woman teacher this same boy may well become the apple of her eye, the model she advises the rest of the class to follow.

The presence of women teachers in the high grades of elementary school and in high school deserves some of the blame for the submissive and immature attitudes of many of our young males. One high school senior, a boy who had been taught almost exclusively by women, commented disgustedly, "The favorite boys in this school are those who are as much like girls as possible. Boys who act like boys find themselves in hot water from the first day of school until the last."

I feel strongly that the education of boys after their ninth or tenth year of age should be in the hands of men. There are many reasons, the main one being that it takes a man to understand a boy's mentality and to judge the boy's actions by masculine standards. All too often, women teachers of pre-adolescent and adolescent boys stress values that women hold high. So the typical boy will go out of his way to prove that he is not the sissy that the teacher's approval of him may suggest.

Boys are often taught by women because not enough men teachers are available. That men are not attracted to the profession of teaching is a serious problem. The quality of all education has lagged because teaching as a profession for either sex has deteriorated in recent years, due in part to the fact that school boards have been more interested in building and maintaining impressive buildings with huge swimming pools, parking lots and innumerable other fringe benefits than in paying attractive salaries.

The special education of boys as boys and girls as girls must go even further. Girls' schools have courses in cooking, sewing and similiar subjects, but it is the rare institution that teaches a girl how to be a wife and mother. Boys may learn how to translate sentences from Latin, but they learn very little about fatherhood.

As another way of strengthening the sense of masculinity or femininity, boys and girls of seventeen or so should not be discouraged from making friends with members of the opposite sex. As a result of such discouragement they may develop undesirable outlets elsewhere. There is a great danger in underestimating the power of the sexual instincts in young people. They have this urge and it must be dealt with. Ideally, it should be sublimated until marriage, and the best way to do this is by using up energy in other stimulating and time-consuming mental and physical activities. Even so, the idea of sex will keep intruding, and if the young person lacks a strong moral motivation, he may find the temptation to engage in some form of sexual activity is beyond his ability to resist. If he is denied normal relationships with the opposite sex, wherein instincts may be partially expressed, and perhaps controlled by idealistic concern for the partner, the sex urge may crop up elsewhere, perhaps in masturbation or in homosexuality. Or it may be repressed to such an extent that a normal sex life will be difficult to achieve even when it becomes morally permissible.

A dominating mother kept telling her college-age son that it was too early to date girls, that they would take his mind off his studies and make it more difficult for him to earn his degree, and furthermore, that girls were an expense he could not afford. After he graduated, she continued to discourage him from dating, on the grounds that girls were a distraction and a luxury that he should forego until he had a better job.

He is now twenty-five years old, lives at home and seems content to do without the companionship of girls. His mother is happy that he has several men friends about the same age, who are quiet and well behaved. In fact, she has often complimented him on the cultured young men he associates with. What she does not know is that she has played an important part in making her son a homosexual, and that his friends are homosexuals too.

Another male homosexual is a professor at a small college along the eastern seaboard. He has spent most of his adult life trying to get out from under his mother's thumb, but even at fifty he has still not succeeded. All through high school his mother forbade dating. He chose a college away from home, hoping he could find a girl friend there, but soon after his first year began, his mother moved to the college town and began to supervise his social relationships. When he introduced her to a few female friends, she found them all highly undesirable in some respect or other. She gave her approval, however, to one boy friend who was always extremely polite to her and considerate of her comforts. Naturally the relationship between mother and son was punctuated by frequent skirmishes in his struggle to free himself and her endeavors to keep him chained.

The overt struggle ceased when the son's relationship with the one approved friend became homosexual. But to escape his mother and his homosexual cravings, the young man decided to enter religious life and—he hoped—miraculously to change his life and his personality. But his biggest problem was where to go so his mother wouldn't follow. He entered a religious order in Europe, but left after a few years because his vocation was more an escape than a reality.

When he returned to the United States, his mother resumed her efforts to dominate him. Much to his relief he was drafted and entered the army, but he had never solved his problem of dependency and he was not really able to cut his psychological umbilical cord. In the army he made new homosexual contacts and lost all interest in developing a normal sexual life.

He is a civilian again, and his mother continues to treat him like a child. She lives only a few miles away from him, visits him several times a week and passes a final judgment on all his actions—his choice of clothes, the way he decorates and maintains his apartment, his choice of food, his friends. Often he actually trembles in fear when he knows she is coming to visit him. Sometimes she stays for a week end, and by Sunday night he literally has to beg her to leave his apartment so that he can do what he wants.

Quite often the influence of the mother more than the father is responsible for the inordinate pressure on young men and women to get into the prestige colleges. No one disputes the value of education nor the fact that young people often need to be encouraged to do their best. Not infrequently, however, young men and women are pushed beyond their endurance and forced into molds which do not fit them. They may get the degree their parents want for them, but at a loss of their own identity.

This pressure results only in part from the mother's desire to give her child the best education in order to prepare him for a successful life. It also arises from the mother's wish to tell friends, relatives and associates that her child is better than the average.

When a youth is accepted by Harvard, Princeton or a similar institution his parents often feel a greater sense of triumph than he does. College students are aware of this pressure. Talk to one in danger of flunking a course, and you are likely to find that his concern is less with his personal failure and more with the fact that his parents, especially his mother, will be unhappy. Thousands—no, hundreds of thousands of youngsters who are now attending classes in institutions of higher learning have no real interest in obtaining an education except that a diploma will get them a better job, provide an entree into the affluent society and make their parents happy.

The pressure on college students is so intense that the rate of nervous breakdowns, emotional disorders and even suicides is tragically high. Less widely recognized is the dramatic effect of scholastic failure on parents. One woman in a well-to-do suburb of New York became intensely distressed because her sixteen-year-old son informed her that he no longer wanted to attend high school. She had known for years that her boy's I.Q. was below average and that great academic success could not be expected of him. But she refused to accept this fact and kept telling him that she wanted him to go to an Ivy League college. He was incapable of doing college work; even many of his high school courses were extremely difficult for him. He wanted to be a racing car driver. He showed a definite aptitude for this career and probably could lead a happy life at it. But when he dropped out of high school his mother never thought of his lack of native intelligence and academic motivation. She ranted and raved at the destruction of all her fondest dreams.

The mother had convinced herself that she was interested in the boy. One day her husband commented that their son would be happier doing what he wanted to do even if he never went to college. Impulsively she blurted out her true feelings. "Oh, sure, it's fine for him. But what about me? When all the neighbors tell me their son is at Harvard or Princeton or studying in Europe, what will I say? That my son is a greasy oil mechanic? How can I hold my head up? You can stick your head in the sand if you want to, but how can I face my friends?"

The point that should be recognized is that, more and more, mothers are taking over the direction of their sons' education not only in the lower grades but through college and even graduate school as well. They stress values which they as women hold high, and as a result, they exert an insistent feminizing influence on their sons.

While we have always had juvenile crime, the problem of juvenile delinquency is greater today than at any time in memory. It is true that four thousand years ago, an Egyptian priest wrote, "Vandalism is rife and crime of all kinds is rampant among our young people." In ancient Athens, Socrates found fault with young people and said that many of them "contradict their parents, gobble up the best at the table and tyrannize over their teachers." Nevertheless, statistical records indicate that the delinquency rate is higher today than ever in the past. An estimate by the Children's Bureau of the United States Department of Labor states that more than 1,100,000 persons under eighteen were arrested in 1962, not including those picked up for traffic violations. Many authorities estimate that for every teen-ager caught committing an act of delinquency, at least two or three get away.

The cause of antisocial behavior in young people and old is a lack of self-esteem. A person who is at ease with his environment and reasonably satisfied with what he is and what he is accomplishing or with the prospects for self-development he sees in the future is not a person who stalks the streets at night seeking victims to mug. The delinquent is one who cannot find a satisfactory answer to the question, Who am I, and where am I going?

Even emotionally secure adolescents are often worried about their ability to lead responsible lives as adults. But such self-doubt assumes monumental proportions when the youth has no clear picture of what will be expected of him as an adult. As I said earlier, when you see a boy who is in serious trouble, you can almost always be sure that he lacks a strong feeling for his father and sense of identification with him. The juvenile delinquent often comes from a broken home not merely because the home is broken, but rather because the strong example of the father is missing. There are many delinquents from homes which are intact but from which the father is a physical or psychological absentee.

Arrests for juvenile delinquency tell only part of the story. The U. S. Public Health Service says there are now approximately 250,000 illegitimate births a year—an increase of 60 percent over the figure ten years ago. The rate has tripled in the last twenty-five years. And the quarter of a million is an understatement, the health service has reported. Some fifteen states do not specifically report illegitimacies. Births to married women are never recorded as illegitimate even when the husband is clearly not the father. And cases of illegitimacy are often concealed by falsifying the records. Moreover, about two million illegal abortions are performed each year, and countless cases of pregnancy out of wedlock are legitimatized by a hasty wedding.

Over 40 percent of the country's unwed mothers are teen-agers.

More than 1,500 pregnant girls under the age of sixteen were dropped from New York City schools in 1963. In Chicago there were known to be 576 pregnant high school or elementary school pupils, including one eleven-year-old girl. In Washington, D.C., schools, there were 265 pregnancies discovered among girls between the ages of twelve and fifteen. In this city one out of every five infants is born to an unwed mother.

Nor is this sex delinquency necessarily the result of slum conditions. In their study of this subject Martin and Marcia Abramson reported that in the maternity homes for unwed mothers run by the Volunteers of America, most girls show surprising intelligence and a good educational background. Few come from families on public assistance. In fact, the greatest percentage increase in illegitimacy is from so-called good families. The pregnant unmarried teen-ager often comes from suburbia, though the facts may be altered in the public records. The Council of School Parents of the well-to-do suburb of Darien, Connecticut, reported recently that there is "an alarming number of pregnancies in high school" there, and "an unbelievable amount of necking and petting involving even youngsters from the sixth and seventh grades." The council quoted a girl student as saying "accepting a date to the drive-in movies is like accepting a date for sex relations." In Westchester County, New York, one of the richest sections in the country, a study revealed a sharp jump in juvenile offenses, including sex delinquency, and in venereal disease, school dropouts and related forms of social behavior. Often these youngsters have everything, except fathers and mothers who are on the job, showing them how to act as men and women.

The prophet's role has always been risky, but in these times of rapid and revolutionary change, it is riskier than ever. Yet one can say with confidence that unless a vigorous effort is made by parents, educators and perhaps most of all by those in control of the opinion-forming apparatus of the modern world, we will continue moving toward a one-sex society, one in which the male might almost as well have been born a female, and vice versa. The movement toward sexual neutrality has become so pronounced in recent years that I can see no evidence of a reversal. On the contrary.

For instance, under the impetus of equal rights legislation, there are no longer jobs that can be considered the exclusive province of the male or the female. The big-muscled Amazon who can wield a baling hook has legally as much right as a male to work as a stevedore. Her sisters have as much right as males to pilot jet airliners or to seek election to the bishopric of some church or other. We have already had women members of the President's cabinet and women senators and representatives, and it seems certain that in the future there will be more rather than fewer. It is not inconceivable that one day we shall see a woman as Chief Justice of the Supreme Court or as President of the United States.

In education most bars have come down, and the few that remain are falling fast. Note the trend led by Harvard and other Ivy League colleges, to open the doors to classrooms once reserved exclusively for men. Examine the vast range of courses offered by modern universities. Women qualify for just about every one. What was once two distinct courses of education, with boys and girls attending separate schools from elementary grades to university, no longer exists.

In parental roles the tendency to sameness is equally pronounced. One need only record the observation of supermarket clerks and laundromat operators, who have seen sharp increases in the number of male customers in recent years. The man who cooked for his family, except in emergencies, once was considered strange indeed; members of the male sex today take pride in an ability to handle a skillet. Some even say it is just as important for a man to be able to cook as it is for his wife.

In sexual roles it is no longer true that the man is the aggressor. It is becoming almost as likely for a girl to phone a boy and suggest a date, to pay half the cost of entertainment (and maybe "lend" him the other half) and to arrange for them to be able to have intercourse later. Moreover, today it is usually the female who is responsible for the effectiveness of the contraceptive.

Outside the home the modern wife is as likely as her husband to represent the family and to present herself as the authority figure. A high school principal commented that when he began to teach forty years ago, if he had trouble with a pupil and demanded to see one of the parents, almost always the father would show up. Today it is equally likely that the mother will appear. At parents' nights, when teachers are available to discuss the work of their pupils, the mothers who appear greatly outnumber fathers.

For a long time now the salesman of everything the family uses, from houses to automobiles to TV sets, has been making his sales appeal primarily to the wife. But now when the sale is made, the wife may well flip out her checkbook and make the payment.

To all of these trends one receives the same reaction from moderns: Why not? If a woman can do a job as well as a man— discipline the children, drive the truck, pay the bills—why not? Unfortunately the problem is not so simple. This trend toward neutrality of the sexes is taking place at a time when evidence is mounting that many of the most serious ills of society stem specifically from the lack of a clear distinction. Science is giving us a mass of evidence that proves how much harm is done to the younger generation by the father who is something less of a man than his own father and by the mother who is less of a woman than her mother. As I have noted, the unwed mother, the homosexual, the alcoholic, the narcotics addict, the husband who cannot accept the responsibilities of marriage, the man and woman unprepared for the ordinary give-and-take of married life—all of these persons more often than not have had a father who was too weak and a mother who was too dominant.

Certainly this should be considered by everyone who helps create opinion—educators, those in command of the communications apparatus, others in positions to influence the public. The schoolteacher who seats a girl student next to a boy and then extols her example should ponder the consequences of his actions. The television script writer who consistently downgrades fathers should realize that the price for a laugh may be too high. The Hollywood producer who gives manly roles in his films to notorious homosexuals should ask himself whether he is as responsible to society as he ought to be.

If you are a parent, you have the power to determine that your child will not become one of the many with lost identities, who lack the example and training they should have received and therefore find themselves in deep personal trouble when they grow up. Since your teaching and example is perhaps the most important single influence in your child's development, you can give him or her the true sense of masculinity or femininity only by developing and emphasizing this sense in yourself. A strong sense of sex is, in the final analysis, a strong sense of self. By giving this to your child you bestow one of the most important gifts within your power to give.

ABOUT THE AUTHOR

DR. ROBERT P. ODENWALD, a practicing psychiatrist for forty years, studied extensively both abroad and in the United States, and was affiliated with many public institutions and organizations. From 1948 to 1953 he was assistant professor of psychiatry at the Catholic University of America. He was a Fellow of the American Medical Association and the American Psychiatric Association, and a Diplomate of the American Board of Psychiatry and Neurology.

Dr. Odenwald was the author of many pamphlets and articles in medical, scientific and Catholic papers, and co-author of the book *Psychiatry and Catholicism* and the author of *Your Child's World*. He was a member of the Advisory Board of the National Academy of Religion and Mental Health.

Dr. Odenwald died shortly before publication. He is survived by his wife and three children.